P9-DCS-281

CRITICAL
ANTHOLOGIES OF
NONFICTION
WRITING™

CRITICAL PERSPECTIVES ON
WORLD WAR I

Edited by
TAMRA ORR

THE ROSEN PUBLISHING GROUP, INC.

NEW YORK

Published in 2005 by The Rosen Publishing Group, Inc.
29 East 21st Street, New York, NY 10010

First Edition

Library of Congress Cataloging-in-Publication Data
Critical perspectives on World War I / edited by Tamra Orr.—
1st ed.
    p. cm.—(Critical anthologies of nonfiction writing)
Includes bibliographical references and index.
ISBN 1-4042-0064-9 (library binding)
1. World War, 1914–1918—Sources. I. Title. II. Series.
D521.C68 2004
940.3—dc22

                                                2004001593

Manufactured in the United States of America

On the cover: Two U.S. soldiers who wear gas masks walk
through billows of smoke during a battle in World War I.

CONTENTS

INTRODUCTION

I f you go into any library or bookstore and browse through the history section, you may be surprised at the lack of materials on World War I. This is always surprising; after all, this was the Great War, the War to End All Wars. Contrary to what the nations thought when it began, it lasted a very long four years. The numbers themselves are staggering: more than 65 million soldiers fought, resulting in more than 21 million injuries and 8 million deaths and a cost of almost $282 billion. So why does it seem there is little written about this tragedy?

The answer is simple: less is generally known about World War I. The First World War was quickly eclipsed by World War II (1939–1945). In fact, some experts believe that they were almost one war, with a twenty-year truce in between. World War II has also been easier for people to understand. It was between good and evil—freedom against the likes of Hitler, Mussolini, and Tojo. The causes of World War I are vague for many people, and understandably so. There hadn't been any major world conflicts for some years, and Europe, in the early 1900s, had the appearance of a cultured, calm, and cooperative collection of nations. People could travel from one place to another freely; commerce was constantly crossing borders as companies did business with each other on a daily basis.

Appearances can be deceiving, however. Underneath all the glitter and polish, preparations for war were being made.

Most of the European nations had arms industries, and all of them, except for Great Britain, had established a compulsory military service and had the ability to move many men quickly and efficiently. Each one of the nations shared the very same thought: eventually war would come and all would be involved when it did.

As peaceful as the nations looked on the surface, this was an illusion. Each country had a plan to gain more power, which most likely could be accomplished only through war. Germany wanted more power. France was eager to get revenge and take back some eastern provinces that Germany had taken earlier. Russia was constantly on the edge of revolution and spoiling for a fight. Great Britain, on the other hand, did not want to go to war but wanted to ensure a stable Europe so that the empire it had created in Asia, Africa, and India could flourish. If it took a war to do that, then so be it. Italy and Turkey were like the rope in the middle of a tug-of-war. They watched and waited as they were pulled in each direction, ready to join the side that seemed the most powerful and offered them the most benefits. All these separate issues were lined up like dominoes, just waiting for that first incident to come along and knock the first tile down. They didn't have to wait long.

The incident began within the Austro-Hungarian Empire. Its leader, Archduke Franz Ferdinand, was assassinated in Sarajevo, Bosnia, by a Serbian. The empire was enraged and wanted to retaliate. Before it did, though, it wanted reassurance from Germany that if Austria-Hungary went to war, Germany would help. Kaiser Wilhelm II of

Germany agreed to do so, and even though Serbia said yes to the list of demands Emperor Franz Josef of Austria sent to it, the decision to go to war was already made. On July 28, 1914, war was officially declared. The dominoes were beginning to topple. No one could have ever dreamed how many years it would take for all of them to fall.

If ever there was a lesson in making and keeping promises, what happened next was it. The finger-pointing began rippling across the land; dominoes fell with crashes that resounded across the planet. After Austria-Hungary declared war on Serbia, Serbia turned to Russia and reminded that country that it had a treaty with Serbia that included Serbia's protection. Russia, keeping its word, mobilized its vast armies to fight. Germany saw this as an act of war, so it declared war on Russia. France had a treaty with Russia also, so it had to join the battle against Germany. Great Britain watched the series of events and waited to see what would happen. Although Great Britain had an agreement with France to protect it in case of war, the agreement was not binding. However, when Germany invaded Belgium—a neutral country that did have a treaty with Great Britain—there were no options left to save the fragile peace. Great Britain joined the fray, and three weeks later, Japan joined in to fight on Great Britain's side.

During those first few months, war was faced not only with courage and determination but also with an almost light-hearted and casual attitude. The summer of 1914 saw more than 6 million young men off to combat, and most of them were smiling. They felt it was going to be a brief skirmish and then they could come home as heroes. Voluntary enlistment was high and so was confidence. After all, how could they lose? Unlike some of history's earlier, rather primitive wars, this new, modern war offered powerful explosives, accurate artillery shells, and improved machine guns, not to mention airplanes for aerial bombing and combat, tanks for rolling over any obstacle, and eventually one of the most devastating weapons—poison gas.

In the beginning, Germany was a powerhouse that seemed unstoppable. It was compared to a giant scythe that cut a 75-mile-wide (121 kilometers wide) swath of death through Belgium and France. When German troops neared Paris, they were exhausted, and France saw its opportunity to strike. For a week, more than 2 million soldiers fought their way to the sea in the Battle of the Marne. It was there that the first inkling of a long-lasting war dawned on leaders. The two sides fought their way to the coast, where they created the trenches that would come to symbolize the inhumanity and futility of the entire conflict. This western front stretched for 600 miles (966 km), and it was home to millions of soldiers for almost four years. The eastern front was also in big trouble. The Schlieffen Plan in the west had not worked out at all like the Germans had hoped; France was not easily defeated and was fighting harder and longer than they had anticipated. This allowed fewer troops available for the battles on the eastern side. While this could have spelled total disaster for the Germans, they were saved by the fact that the Russians were slow moving and had inadequate training and supplies.

The war went on for years, with little progress on either side except for more injuries and deaths. In 1917, the entire picture changed, however. Until now, it had been Great Britain, France, and Russia (the Allies) against Germany, Austria-Hungary, and Turkey (the Central Powers). Two things altered the scenario. Russia, through revolution, had switched governments and the new rulers made peace with Germany. To show their newfound allegiance, they joined the war on the side of the Central powers. Immediately, the balance shifted.

Eyes turned to the United States. What would it do now? Could the United States possibly remain neutral? The domino that tipped over and forced America's involvement came from the sea. For more than two years, Germany's U-boats (submarines) had been sinking hundreds of ocean liners, including the *Lusitania*. Thousands of people had drowned, many of them Americans. At first, President Woodrow Wilson simply cut off diplomatic relations with Germany, but as these sinkings continued and the nation's people got angrier, he knew more action was necessary. The discovery of the Zimmerman telegram proposing an alliance between Germany and Mexico was the tipping point. On April 2, 1917, the United States officially joined the war.

It took time to marshal enough troops and get them to where they were needed along the front. In the spring of 1918, 2 million American soldiers marched off to join a four-year-old war. These troops were fresh, young, healthy, and enthusiastic; they made all the difference. In less than a month, these "Yanks" had recaptured Borsches, Vaux, and Belleau Wood. In a second Battle of the Marne, 85,000 American troops broke the western front's deadlock and defeated Germany. It was the turning point of the war. The United States went on to lead victories at many more battlefields. And in September, 1.2 million U.S. soldiers cut off Germany's supply lines, effectively ending the war.

The armistice became official on the eleventh hour of the eleventh day of the eleventh month of 1918. The goals and intentions of the Treaty of Versailles were idealistic but, in the end, ineffective. Although papers were signed and celebrations were held, Britain, France, and Italy walked away vowing revenge on Germany. Because of the harsh requirements of the treaty, Germany was plunged into a period of economic, political, and social doom, which the people deeply resented and which would feed the fires of their fury. Twenty years later, these countries would all come face-to-face again and the temporary truce would be over. The War to End All Wars would serve as a prologue to the bigger war to come. The line of falling dominoes was far from being finished.

This anthology offers a unique perspective on this era in history because it encompasses so many different perspectives on the war. It takes you inside the minds of individual soldiers and rulers, the powerful and the powerless. It brings into focus the cultures of people and places from a time gone by and shows how the world has—and has not—changed. Moreover, the anthology teaches how science, government, communities, and people had to work together to survive the long and difficult battle that was World War I.

CHAPTER ONE

POWER, AUTHORITY, AND GOVERNANCE: THE ARMIES OF EUROPE IN 1914

"Europe 1914"
From The Lessons of History
By Sir Michael Howard
1991

The Europe of 1914 was much like a mirage in the middle of a desert. It looked comfortable and pleasant from far away, but the closer someone got, the more transparent the illusion became and reality shone through. Outwardly, the nations of Europe were calm, but inwardly, there was turmoil and a certainty of—even a desire for—war. Many people of the time, including politicians, equated war not with devastation, death, and destruction, but with honor, nobility, and as a necessary struggle for a nation if progress is to be made.

Even though war was rarely spoken of out loud, multiple preparations for it were under way in every one of the nations. This selection from esteemed historian Sir Michael Howard takes a close look at that unique period in history in Europe, when the mood of the people and the politicians

appeared peaceful and placid, but in reality, were churning
and waiting to declare war.

———□———

Let us begin where the war itself effectively began, in
Vienna. Was not the prospect that lay before the statesmen
of Vienna, even if this crisis were successfully "managed,"
one of continuous frustration abroad and disintegration at
home? Of a Serbia, doubled in size after the Balkan Wars,
ever more boldly backing the claims of the Bosnian irreden-
tists, while other South Slavs agitated with ever greater confidence for an autonomy that the empire would never permit
them to exercise? What serious prospect was there of the
empire hanging together once the old emperor had gone? A
final settling of accounts with Serbia while Germany held
the Russians in check must have seemed the only chance of
saving the monarchy, whatever Berlin might say; and with a
blank check from Berlin, Vienna could surely face the future
with a greater confidence than had been felt there for very
many years. No wonder Count Leopold von Berchtold and his
colleagues took their time drafting their ultimatum: They
must have found the process highly enjoyable. A successful
war would put the monarchy back in business again, and
keep it there for many years to come.

What about the government in Berlin? Was this the
moment it had been waiting for ever since the huge expansion
of the army resulting from the famous Council of War in
December 1912? The controversy about this has consumed
many tons of paper and gallons of ink. But if one asks again

what the imperial German government had to lose by peace and gain by war, the answers seem very clear. One of the things it had to lose by peace was its Austrian ally, which would become an increasingly useless burden as it grew ever less capable of solving its internal problems or protecting its own (and German) interests in the Balkans against the encroachments of Russia and Russia's protégés.

Another thing Germany stood to lose was her capacity to hold her own against a dual alliance in which French capital was building up a Russian army whose future size and mobility appeared far beyond the capability of any German force to contain. It would not be too anachronistic to suggest that the shadow of Russia's future status as a superpower was already rendering out of date all calculations based on the traditional concept of a European balance. If war was to come at all— and few people in the imperial government doubted that it would—then it was self-evidently better to have it now, while there was still a fair chance of victory. By 1917, when the Russians had completed the great program of rearmament and railway building that they had begun, with French funding, in 1912, it might be too late.

And, for Germany, there was a lot to be gained by war. The domination of the Balkans and perhaps the Middle East; the final reduction of France to a position from which she could never again, even with allies, pose a military threat to German power; the establishment of a position on the Continent that would enable Germany to compete on equal terms with England and attain the grandiose if ill-defined status of a world power—all this, in July 1914, must have appeared perfectly feasible. In September, when the program of her war aims was drafted, it looked as if it had almost been achieved. Even in a less bellicose and more self-confident society than Wilhelmine Germany, the opportunity might have seemed too good to miss.

In Vienna and Berlin then, there seemed much to be lost by peace and gained by war. In St. Petersburg, the ambitions for Balkan expansion and the "recovery" of Constantinople, which had been checked in 1878 and 1885, were far from dead, but they can hardly be considered a major element in Russian political calculations in July 1914. More serious were the costs of remaining at peace: abandoning Serbia and all the gains of the past five years; facing the wrath of the Pan-Slavs in the Duma and their French allies; and watching the Central Powers establish and consolidate an unchallengeable dominance in southeast Europe. Even so, these costs were hardly irredeemable. Russia had been humiliated before in the Balkans and had been able to restore her authority. She had no vital interests there that, once lost, could never be recovered. Above all, she had nothing to lose in terms of military power by waiting, and a great deal to gain. Of all the major European powers, Russia's entry into the war can be categorized as the least calculated, the most unwise, and ultimately, of course, the most disastrous.

As for Paris and London, a successful war would certainly remove—as it ultimately did—a major threat to their security. But the advantages to be gained by war did not enter into their calculations, whereas the perils of remaining at peace evidently did. The French government took little comfort from the long-term advantages to be gained from the growth of Russian military power and paid little heed to the consequent advisability of postponing the issue until 1917. It was more conscious of its immediate weakness in the face of the growing German army. In 1914, after the increase of the past two years, German peacetime strength had reached 800,000 men, its wartime strength 3.8 million.

Thanks to their new and controversial Three-Year Law, the French could match this with 700,000 men in peace, 3.5 million in war. But with a population of only 60 percent of the Germans', that was almost literally their final throw. Completion of the Russian reforms was three years away. In the long run Russian strength might redress the balance, but in the long run a large number of Frenchmen could be dead and their nation reduced to the status of Italy or Spain. So the French government saw no reason to urge caution on St. Petersburg, and even less reason to refrain from supporting its ally when Germany declared war on her on August 1.

To the British government, composed largely (although by no means entirely) of men to whom the whole idea of war was antipathetic and who were responsible to a parliamentary party deeply suspicious of militarism and of Continental involvement, there appeared nothing to be gained by war. Indeed, perhaps more than any of its Continental equivalents, the British government was conscious of the possible costs, but was equally conscious of the cost of remaining at peace. She had no demands to make on any of the belligerents, no territorial aspirations, no expectation of economic gain. So far as the British government was concerned, Norman Angell's famous book *The Great Illusion* was preaching to the converted. But if the Dual Alliance defeated Germany unaided, the two victors would regard Britain with hostility and contempt. All the perils of imperial rivalry that were temporarily dispersed by the Entente with France in 1904 and the British accords with Russia of 1907 would reappear. If, on the other hand, Germany won and established a Continental hegemony, Britain would face a threat to her security unknown since the days of Napoleon.

Leaving aside any consideration of honor, sentiment, or respect for treaties—and let us remember that that generation of Englishmen did not leave them aside but regarded them as quite central—every consideration of real politik dictated that Britain, having done her best to avert the war, should enter it on the side of France and Russia once it began.

When the statesmen of Europe declared war in 1914, they all shared one assumption: that they had a better-than-even chance of winning it. In making this assumption they relied on their military advisers, so it is now time to look at our second element in the triad: the soldiers.

The first thing to note about the soldiers—certainly those of western Europe—is that they were professionals, and most of them professionals of a very high order. Those of them who were wellborn or socially ambitious certainly shared the feudal value system so excoriated by Professor Arno Mayer in his book *The Persistence of the Old Regime*. Those who were not probably had more than their fair share of the prevalent philosophy of social Darwinism and regarded war not as an unpleasant necessity but as a test of manhood and of national fitness for survival. In all armies, then as now, there were incompetents who through good luck or good connections reached unsuitably high rank; but a study of the military literature of the period strongly indicates that the military professionals—especially those responsible for the armament, training, organization, and deployment of armies—were no fools, worked hard, and took their jobs very seriously. And they, too, shared certain assumptions.

The first was that war was inevitable. The now much-quoted statement made by General Helmuth von Moltke (namesake of his famous uncle) at the so-called Council of War in December 1912, "I hold war to be inevitable, and the sooner the better," can be paralleled with comparable expressions by responsible figures in every army in Europe. They may have differed over the second part of the sentence— whether it was better to get it over with quickly or wait for a more favorable moment—but from 1911 onward it is hard to find any military leader suggesting that war could or should be avoided any longer . . .

The extent to which war was generally regarded as inevitable or desirable by the public as a whole is still difficult to gauge—although if the "distant drummer" penetrated into the summer idylls of A. E. Housman's poetry, it is reasonable to suppose that less remote figures found the sound pretty deafening. Certainly the evidence is overwhelming that the question in military minds was not "whether" but "when." They saw their job as being not to deter war but to fight it.

The second assumption, which they shared with the statesmen they served, was that the war would be short. It required exceptional perspicacity to visualize anything else. Ivan Bloch, in his work *La Guerre Future*, published in 1898, had forecast with amazing accuracy that the power of modern weapons would produce deadlock on the battlefield and that the resulting attrition would destroy the fabric of the belligerent societies. Bloch's thesis was widely known and much discussed in military periodicals. But since he was saying in effect that the military was now faced with a problem it could not solve, it was unlikely that many soldiers would agree with him . . .

Finally, we must remember that the stalemate on the Western Front did not develop for six months, and that on the Eastern Front it never developed at all. The open warfare of maneuver for which the armies of Europe had prepared was precisely what, in the autumn of 1914, they got. It resulted in a succession of spectacular German victories in eastern Europe, and given bolder and more flexible leadership it might very well have done the same in the west. The terrible losses suffered by the French in Alsace in August and by the British and Germans in Flanders in November came in encounter battles, not in set-piece assaults against prepared defensive positions; and they were losses that, to the military leadership at least, came as no great surprise.

For this was the final assumption shared by soldiers throughout Europe: that in any future war, armies would have to endure very heavy losses indeed. The German army, for one, had never forgotten the price it paid for its victories in 1870, when the French had been armed with breech-loading rifles that, in comparison with the weapons now available, were primitive. Since then the effects of every new weapon had been studied with meticulous care, and no professional soldier was under any illusions about the damage that would be caused—not simply by machine guns (which were in fact seen as ideal weapons of a mobile offensive) but by magazine-loading rifles and by quick-firing artillery hurling shrapnel at infantry in the open and high explosives against trenches. Their effects had been studied through controlled experiment and also in action, in the South African and Russo-Japanese Wars. The conclusion generally drawn was that in the future, infantry would be able to advance only in open formations, making use of all available cover, under the protection of con-centrated artillery fire . . .

This brings us belatedly to the third element in the triad, the people. Without the support, or at least the acquiescence, of the peoples of Europe, there would have been no war. This is the most interesting and most complex area for historians to investigate. We know a lot—almost to excess—about the mood of the intellectuals and the elites in 1914, but what about the rest? . . .

What does appear self-evident is that the doubts many European leaders felt about the morale of their peoples proved in 1914 to be ill-founded. Those who welcomed war with enthusiasm may have been a minority concentrated in the big cities, but those who opposed it were probably a smaller minority still. The vast majority were willing to do what their governments expected of them. Nationalistically oriented public education; military service that, however unwelcome and tedious, bred a sense of cohesion and national identity; continuous habits of social deference—all of this helps explain, at a deeper level than does the strident propaganda of the popular press, why the populations of Europe responded so readily to the call when it came. The war came as an escape from humdrum or intolerable lives into a world of adventure and comradeship . . .

Probably only a tiny minority considered the idea of war in itself repellent. Few military historians, and no popular historians, had yet depicted the realities of the battlefield in their true horror, and only a few alarmist prophets could begin to conceive what the realities of future battlefields would be like. Their nations, so the peoples of Europe had learned at school, had achieved their present greatness through successful wars—the centenaries of the Battles of Trafalgar and Leipzig had recently been celebrated with great enthusiasm in Great Britain and Germany and there was no reason to think that they would not one day have to fight again. Military leaders were everywhere respected and popular; military music was an intrinsic part of popular culture. In the popular mind, as in the military mind, wars were seen not as terrible evils to be deterred but as necessary struggles to be fought and won . . .

"28 June, 1914: The Assassination of Archduke Franz Ferdinand"
By Borijove Jevtic
1914

When World War I began, it was much like a series of dominoes tipping over onto each other. The momentum to start them falling had been there for some time, but the event that focused that power and knocked over the first domino was the murder of Archduke Franz Ferdinand. He was a man who liked titles and the authority they imparted. As Archduke of Austria and inspector general of the Austro-Hungarian army, he secretly longed to add king of Slavs, emperor of Austria, and king of Hungary to the list. When his empire claimed Bosnia, he decided to take a trip to visit the country's capital, a little-known place at the time called Sarajevo. This selection comes from one of the assassins himself, Borijove Jevtic, a leader of the Narodna Odbrana, whose written confession presents a comment seldom seen in history: the view of a murderer.

A tiny clipping from a newspaper, mailed without comment from a secret band of terrorists in Zagreb, capital of Croatia, to their comrades in Belgrade, was the torch which set the world afire with war in 1914. That bit of paper wrecked old, proud empires. It gave birth to new, free nations.

I was one of the members of the terrorist band in Belgrade which received it.

The little clipping declared that the Austrian Archduke Francis Ferdinand would visit Sarajevo, the capital of Bosnia, June 28, to direct army maneuvers in the neighboring mountains.

It reached our meeting place, the cafe called Zlatna Moruna, one night the latter part of April, 1914. To understand how great a sensation that little piece of paper caused among us when it was passed from hand to hand almost in silence, and how greatly it inflamed our hearts, it is necessary to explain just why the Narodna Odbrana existed, the kind of men that were in it, and the significance of that date, June 28, on which the Archduke dared to enter Sarajevo.

As every one knows, the old Austrio-Hungarian Empire was built by conquest and intrigues, by sales and treacheries, which held [. . .] men of the upper classes were ardent patriots. They were dissimilar in everything except hatred of the oppressor.

Such were the men into whose hands the tiny bit of newsprint was sent by friends in Bosnia that April night in Belgrade. At a small table in a very humble cafe, beneath a flickering gas jet we sat and read it. There was no advice nor admonition sent with it. Only four letters and two numerals were sufficient to make us unanimous, without discussion, as to what we should do about it.

They were conived [sic] in Sarajevo all the twenty-two conspirators were in their allotted positions, armed and ready. They were distributed five hundred yards apart over the whole route along which the Archduke must travel from the railroad station to the town hall.

When Francis Ferdinand and his retinue drove from the station they were allowed to pass the first two conspirators. The motor cars were driving too fast to make an attempt feasible and in the crowd were many Serbians; throwing a grenade would have killed many innocent people.

When the car passed Gabrinovic, the compositor, he threw his grenade. It hit the side of the car, but Francis Ferdinand with presence of mind threw himself back and was uninjured. Several officers riding in his attendance were injured.

The cars sped to the Town Hall and the rest of the conspirators did not interfere with them. After the reception in the Town Hall General Potiorek, the Austrian Commander, pleaded with Francis Ferdinand to leave the city, as it was seething with rebellion. The Archduke was persuaded to drive the shortest way out of the city and to go quickly.

The road to the maneuvers was shaped like the letter *V*, making a sharp turn at the bridge over the River Milgacka. Francis Ferdinand's car could go fast enough until it reached this spot but here it was forced to slow down for the turn. Here Princip had taken his stand.

As the car came abreast he stepped forward from the curb, drew his automatic pistol from his coat and fired two shots. The first struck the wife of the Archduke, the Archduchess Sofia, in the abdomen. She was an expectant mother. She died instantly.

The second bullet struck the Archduke close to the heart.

He uttered only one word, "Sofia"— a call to his stricken wife. Then his head fell back and he collapsed. He died almost instantly.

The officers seized Princip. They beat him over the head with the flat of their swords. They knocked him down, they kicked him, scraped the skin from his neck with the edges of their swords, tortured him, all but killed him.

The next day they put chains on Princip's feet, which he wore till his death . . .

I was placed in the cell next to Princip's, and when Princip was taken out to walk in the prison yard I was taken along as his companion . . .

Awakened in the middle of the night and told that he was to be carried off to another prison, Princip made an appeal to the prison governor:

"There is no need to carry me to another prison. My life is already ebbing away. I suggest that you nail me to a cross and burn me alive. My flaming body will be a torch to light my people on their path to freedom."

"Who's Who"
From http://www.firstworldwar.com
By Michael Duffy
2001

There were many different influential commanders in Germany's army, but three of the most well known were Paul von Hindenburg, Erich Ludendorff, and Count Alfred von Schlieffen.

Paul von Hindenburg acted as field marshal during the First World War. In the following war, he helped the Nazis rise to power and would help Adolf Hitler on his pathway of destruction.

Erich Ludendorff was the chief of staff to Germany's Second Army. He was put into power when the chief officer of Germany's Fourteenth Brigade was killed in action and a replacement was needed immediately.

Schlieffen was chief of general staff and the man responsible for the meticulously planned, obsessively thought-out Schlieffen Plan. It was a detailed war plan of attack that Germany would adopt wholeheartedly. It was also a plan that certainly did not work out like it was supposed to. All three men would play important roles within the war and within history itself each in their own ways.

---□---

Paul von Hindenburg

Paul von Beneckendorff und von Hindenburg (1847–1934) was born in Poznan on 2 October 1847, the eldest of three sons, and was educated at cadet schools in Wahlstatt and Berlin.

He first saw military action at the Battle of Koniggratz in 1866 and in the Franco-Prussian War of 1870–71. He was subsequently appointed to the General Staff in 1878, reaching General rank in 1905. He married Gertrud von Sperling in 1879 while stationed at Strettin; they had three children, a boy and two girls.

Hindenburg retired from the army 1911. The outbreak of the First World War led to his inevitable recall on 22 August 1914, being sent to the Eastern Front as Commander of East Prussia. The Germans scored a notable victory at Tannenberg in August 1914, where Hindenburg overcame a much larger army, leading to his appointment as

Commander-in-Chief of the German armies in the East in September 1914.

Further victory at the Masurian Lakes in 1915 resulted in his being hailed as the saviour of East Prussia, although his Chief of Staff Erich Ludendorff—who held this position with Hindenburg throughout the war, remaining a close ally— is generally credited for achieving these victories.

Hindenburg was consequently promoted to Field Marshal, finally becoming Army Chief of Staff on 29 August 1916, succeeding the man with whom he'd violently disagreed with concerning Eastern policy, Erich Falkenhayn, and whose downfall he had helped to engineer. He immediately appointed Ludendorff his Quartermaster General.

Now in a position of power, Hindenburg, in conjunction with Erich Ludendorff, and with the support of senior officers and prominent industrialists, formed what was known as the "Third Supreme Council," a military-industrial dictatorship that held virtually total power until 29 September 1918 when, with defeat inevitable, power was returned to the Reichstag.

Whilst Chief of Staff Hindenburg, again largely acting under Ludendorff's direction, managed to stem the Allied advance on the Western Front, and consolidated the formidable Hindenburg Line, which ran from Lens through Saint-Quentin to Reims. Romania was quickly defeated after discarding its neutrality and entering the war on the side of the Allies; and Russia was forced out of the war in 1917.

Hindenburg oversaw the final great German push of spring 1918 in France, which ran from March to July. A costly offensive, it almost succeeded. However an Allied counter-offensive, bolstered by the arrival of U.S. troops, broke through, forcing German surrender in November 1918.

A popular hero, Hindenburg retired once again from the German army in June 1919, but remained in office. Under the terms of the Treaty of Versailles Hindenburg was due to be tried as a war criminal; however his popularity ensured that he was not even indicted.

Hindenburg became President of the Weimar Republic in 1925, replacing Friedrich Ebert upon the latter's death, achieving re-election in 1932. Hindenburg, by then virtually senile, was responsible for appointing Adolf Hitler Chancellor in 1933, fearing civil war otherwise.

Such was Hindenburg's popularity that Hitler chose not to remove Hindenburg from office, preferring instead to wait for his death, on 2 August 1934, at which point constitutional government was disbanded.

Erich Ludendorff

Erich Ludendorff (1865–1937) was born near Poznan on 9 April 1865.

Commissioned into the infantry in 1883 and a member of the General Staff from 1894, Ludendorff served as head of the deployment section in 1908. A highly militaristic man, Ludendorff held that peace was merely the interval between wars, and that the nation's chief duty was to provide the means with which to conduct war. In the pre-war period Ludendorff assisted with the fine-tuning of the invasion strategy for France, the Schlieffen Plan.

Upon the outbreak of the First World War he was made quartermaster general to von Bulow's Second Army, responsible for capturing the Liege forts, without which the Schlieffen Plan could not succeed. This task successfully accomplished, Ludendorff was sent to East Prussia where he worked with Paul von Hindenburg as his Chief of Staff.

Hindenburg, who relied heavily upon Ludendorff in crafting his victories at Tannenberg (1914) and the Masurian Lakes (1915), later appointed Ludendorff his quartermaster general when he was appointed Chief of Staff of the German Army in late August 1916, replacing Erich Falkenhayn.

Shortly after becoming Chief of Staff, Hindenburg, working with Ludendorff and leading industrialists, created what was effectively a military-industrial dictatorship, the Third Supreme Command, largely relegating the Kaiser, Wilhelm II, to a peripheral role. Ludendorff was the chief engineer behind the management of the German war effort during this time, with Hindenburg his pliant front man.

Ludendorff was a supporter of unrestricted submarine warfare, an especially controversial policy with the then-neutral Americans, ultimately responsible for bringing the U.S. into the war. An aggressive commander, Ludendorff pressured the Kaiser to dismiss those in the armed forces who favoured a negotiated peace settlement; Wilhelm agreed, with Chancellor Bethmann-Hollweg a casualty of Ludendorff's "defeatist" campaign.

With Russia's withdrawal from the war in 1917, Ludendorff played a key role in the Brest-Litovsk peace treaty, an agreement negotiated at great cost to Russia.

Expecting a successful resolution to the great German spring push in 1918, Ludendorff realised that the war was lost once the offensive failed, aware that with the arrival of fresh American troops the impetus would quickly swing to the Allies. He therefore, with Hindenburg, transferred power back to the Reichstag on 29 September, demanding an immediate peace; subsequently changing his mind, Ludendorff was forced to resign on 26 October under pressure from Max von Baden's government.

With the armistice Ludendorff left Germany for Sweden. Whilst in exile he wrote numerous books and articles mythologizing the German military's conduct of the war, claiming that the army had been "stabbed in the back" by Germany's left-wing political element.

Ludendorff eventually returned to Germany in 1920, where as a right-wing politician he took part in the Hitler Munich Putsch of 9 November 1923. In 1924 he was elected to the Reichstag as a representative of the Nazi party, serving until 1928. He contested the 1925 presidential election against his former commander, Paul von Hindenburg, the latter easily winning.

Erich Ludendorff died on 20 December 1937 at the age of 72. Hitler attended his funeral.

Alfred von Schlieffen

Alfred von Schlieffen (1833–1913) was the German Field Marshal who, as chief of the general staff from 1891–1905, was responsible for devising the Schlieffen Plan, upon which

German strategy at the outbreak of the war was unsuccessfully based. Debate continues today as to whether the plan itself was flawed, or whether its execution was flawed.

Schlieffen, born on 28 February 1833, was the son of a Prussian general, and entered the army himself in 1854. Quickly moving to the general staff he participated in the Seven Weeks War against Austria in 1866 and in the Franco-Prussian War of 1870–71.

In 1884 Schlieffen became head of the military history section of the general staff, replacing Alfred, Graf von Waldersee as chief of the Great General Staff in 1891.

The Schlieffen Plan provided for a war on two fronts, West and East, by first quickly defeating France through a concentration of troops on the Western Front, which by moving rapidly through Belgium and Holland would defeat France in a flanking movement (overwhelmingly so on its right). Meanwhile a smaller army would hold off Russia in the east.

The plan disregarded Belgian and Dutch neutrality and required boldness in its execution. Once war actually broke out the plan was initiated in a modified form, but a number of factors led to its failure, including German lack of mobility, increased Russian numbers, effective French resistance— and the reluctance of Schlieffen's successor, Helmuth von Moltke, to weaken his Eastern Front.

During World War Two a variation of the Schlieffen Plan was again employed by Germany which, in the absence of Russian opposition, proved successful.

Alfred von Schlieffen died on 4 January 1913 in Berlin.

"When you march into France, let the last man on the right brush the Channel with his sleeve"

—Referring to the Schlieffen Plan

"The Crisis of 1914"
From **The First World War**
by John Keegan
1999

Before matters came to a head in 1914, Otto von Bismarck, who reshaped Europe and unified Germany in 1871, was quoted as saying that war would explode one day because of "some damn foolish thing in the Balkans." Later events proved him right.

Diplomacy had failed, Franz Ferdinand was dead, and Count Leopold von Berchtold, Austria-Hungary's foreign minister, pointed the finger of guilt at Serbia. He saw the opportunity to repress the building strength and drive of Bosnia and Serbia and to bring much-needed honor to the Austro-Hungarian Empire. Berchtold turned to Germany to ask for its backing in a war. During a luncheon, the kaiser casually agreed to support Austria-Hungary, suspecting that little would ever come of it because certainly Serbia would give in to whatever demands Austria presented. His mistake would soon affect the world.

John Keegan examines the days leading up to the Great War. As it became known later, there was ample opportunity to stop the war, but countries were jealous of one another, their treaties forced moves that would never be accepted today, and face-saving came at a heavy price.

———□———

Secret plans determined that any crisis not settled by sensible diplomacy would, in the circumstances prevailing in Europe in 1914, lead to general war. Sensible diplomacy had settled crises before, notably during the powers' quarrels over position in Africa and in the disquiet raised by the Balkan Wars of 1912–13. Such crises, however, had touched matters of national interest only, not matters of national honour or prestige. In June 1914 the honour of Austria-Hungary, most sensitive because weakest of European powers, was touched to the quick by the murder of the heir to the throne at the hands of an assassin who identified himself with the monarchy's most subversive foreign neighbour. The Austro-Hungarian empire, a polity of five major religions and a dozen languages, survived in dread of ethnic subversion. The chief source of subversion was Serbia, an aggressive, backward and domestically violent Christian kingdom which had won its independence from the rule of the Muslim Ottoman empire after centuries of rebellion. Independent Serbia did not include all Serbs. Large minorities remained, by historical accident, Austrian subjects. Those who were nationalists resented rule by the Habsburgs almost as much as their free brothers had rule by the Ottomans. The most extreme among them were prepared to kill. It was the killing by one of them of the Habsburg heir that fomented the fatal crisis of the summer of 1914.

The Habsburg army's summer manoeuvres of 1914 were held in Bosnia, the former Ottoman Turkish province occupied by Austria in 1878 and annexed to the empire in 1908. Franz Ferdinand, nephew to the Emperor Franz Josef and Inspector General of the army, arrived in Bosnia on 25 June to supervise. After the manoeuvres concluded, on 27 June, he drove next morning with his wife to the provincial capital, Sarajevo, to carry out official engagements. It was an ill-chosen day: 28 June is the anniversary of the defeat of Serbia by the Turks in 1389, Vidov Dan, the event from which they date their long history of suffering at the hands of foreign oppressors. The archducal couple's chauffeur took a wrong turning and, while reversing, came to a momentary halt. The stop brought the car opposite one of the undetected conspirators, Gavrilo Princip, who was armed with a revolver. He stepped forward and fired. The Archduke's wife died instantly, he ten minutes later. Princip was arrested on the spot.

Investigation swiftly revealed that, though the terrorists were all Austrian subjects, they had been armed in Serbia and smuggled back across the Austrian border by a Serbian nationalist organisation. The Austrian investigators identified it as the *Narodna Odbrana* (National Defence), set up in 1908 to work against the incorporation of Bosnia into the Austrian empire; it was a tenet of the nationalist creed that Bosnia was historically Serb . . .

The evidence of Serb complicity, official or not, in the assassination of Franz Ferdinand, exposed by the conspirators' confessions of 2 July, was therefore enough to persuade many in the imperial government that a war against Serbia was now a necessity. As it happened, Count Berchtold, the Austro-Hungarian Foreign Minister, had spent much of the week before the assassination preparing aggressive diplomatic measures against Serbia. His scheme was to persuade Germany to support Austria in seeking an alliance with Bulgaria and Turkey, Serbia's enemies in the Second Balkan War of 1913, which would confront the Belgrade government with a hostile encirclement: Bulgaria and Turkey to the east, Austria-Hungary to the west and north. The assassination lent urgency to Berchtold's diplomacy. An Austrian emissary was ordered to Berlin with the document in early July. On 4 July, the eve of his departure, Berchtold made radical amendments to it. The memorandum now requested the German government to recognise that the empire's differences with Serbia were "irreconcilable" and stated the "imperious . . . necessity for the Monarchy [Austria-Hungary] to destroy with a determined hand the net which its enemies are attempting to draw over its head." A covering letter alleged that "the Sarajevo affair . . . was the result of a well-organised conspiracy, the threads of which can be traced to Belgrade" and insisted that "the pivot of the Panslavic policy" (Serbia as the protagonist of a "Greater Serbia") "must be eliminated as a power factor in the Balkans." Berchtold gave the emissary, Count Hoyos, verbal authority to warn the Germans that Vienna would ask Belgrade for guarantees as to its future conduct, to be followed by military action if refused. Within six days of the assassination, therefore, Austria had staked out her position.

It remained to see whether the German Emperor and his government, without whose backing the Austrians dare not act, would support them . . .

Had Austria moved at once, without seeking Germany's endorsement, it is possible, perhaps probable, that the Serbs would have found themselves as isolated strategically as, initially, they were morally, and so forced to capitulate to the Austrian ultimatum. It was Austria's unwillingness to act unilaterally that transformed a local into a general European crisis and her unwillingness to act must be explained in large part by the precautionary mood of thought which decades of contingent war planning had implanted in the mind of European governments.

The net of interlocking and opposed understandings and mutual assistance treaties—France to go to war on Russia's side and vice versa if either were attacked by Germany, Britain to lend assistance to France if the vital interests of both were judged threatened, Germany, Austria-Hungary and Italy (the Triple Alliance) to go to war together if any one were attacked by two other states—is commonly held to have been the mechanism which brought the "Allies" (France, Russia and Britain) into conflict in 1914 with the "Central Powers" (Germany and Austria-Hungary). Legalistically that cannot be denied. It was no treaty, however, that caused Austria to go running to Berlin for guidance and support in the aftermath of the Sarajevo assassination—no treaty in any case applied—but anticipation of the military consequences that might ensue should she act alone. At their worst, those consequences would bring Russia to threaten Austria on their common border as a warning to desist from action against Serbia; Austria would then look to Germany for support; that support, if given, risked drawing France into the crisis as a counterweight against German pressure on Russia; the combination of France and Russia would supply the circumstances to activate the Triple Alliance (with or without Italy); the ingredients of a general European war would then be in place. In short, it was the calculation of presumed military response, of how it was guessed one military precaution would follow from another, that drove Austria to seek comfort in the Triple Alliance from the outset, not the Triple Alliance that set military events in train . . .

[On] the twenty-fifth day since the assassination the Serbian government had been warned that the note was on its way. Nicholas Pasic, the Serbian Prime Minister, had nevertheless decided to leave the capital for the country and, even after word reached him that the Austrian ambassador had brought the document to the foreign ministry, proceeded with his journey. Only during the night did he decide to return and it was not until ten o'clock in the morning of Friday 24 July that he met his ministers to consider what answer should be made. The Russian, German and British governments had already received their copies of the text, and so had the French though, with the President and Foreign Minister still at sea, in Paris it was in the hands of a deputy. In Belgrade, however, the British minister was ill, the Russian minister had just died and not been replaced, while a replacement for the French minister, who had had a nervous breakdown, had only just arrived. The Serbian ministry were thus deprived of experienced diplomatic advice at a moment when the need was critical. Belgrade was a small and remote city, and the government, though experienced in the rough-and-ready diplomacy of Balkan warfare, was ill-equipped to deal with a crisis likely to involve all the great powers. The Serbian ministers, moreover, had taken fright as they pored over the Austrian note in the absence of Pasic. On his return, though there was some bold, initial talk of war, the mood quickly moved towards acquiescence. Messages were received from Sir Edward Grey, the British Foreign Minister, and from Paris, both counselling acceptance of as much of the Austrian note as possible. By the following morning, Saturday 25 July, both the British and French delegations in Belgrade reported home that Belgrade would agree to the Austrian demands, excepting the condition that imperial officials be admitted on to Serbian territory to supervise the investigations.

Even on that sticking point, however, the Serbians had as yet not made up their minds. As late as the twenty-seventh day after the assassination, it therefore seemed possible that Austria would arrive at the result it might very well have achieved had it exercised its right as a sovereign power to move against Serbia from the outset. The vital interest of no other power was threatened, except by consideration of prestige, even if Serbia permitted Austrian officials to participate in judicial proceedings conducted on its territory. That would be a humiliation to the Serbs, and a violation of the idea of sovereignty by which the states of Europe conducted relations between themselves. Yet, given Serbia's semi-rogue status in the international community, it was unlikely to constitute an issue of principle for others, unless others made that choice. Even at noon on Saturday 25 July, therefore, five hours before the time limit attached to the Austrian note would expire, the crime of Sarajevo remained a matter between Austria-Hungary and Serbia, diplomatically no more than that.

Such was strictly true in the arena of diplomatic protocol. In the real world, however, the elapse of three weeks and six days since the murders had given time for fears to fester, premonitions to take form, positions to be taken in outline. . . .

On the morning of 25 July they were still reconciled to capitulation, though reluctantly and with occasional bursts of belligerence. Then, during the afternoon, word was received from their ambassador at the Tsar's country palace that the mood there was fiercely pro-Serbian. The Tsar, though not yet ready to proclaim mobilisation, had announced the preliminary "Period Preparatory to War" at eleven o'clock. The news reversed everything the Serbian ministers had decided. In the morning they had agreed to accept all ten Austrian demands, with the slightest reservations. Now they were emboldened to attach conditions to six and to reject absolutely the most important, that Austrian officials be allowed to take part in the investigation of the assassinations on Serbian territory. In the hurried hours that followed, the reply to the note was drafted and redrafted lines crossed out, phrases corrected in ink. As would happen in the Japanese embassy in Washington on the night before Pearl Harbor, the typist gave way to nerves. The finished document was an undiplomatic palimpsest of revisions and afterthoughts. With a quarter of an hour in hand, however, it was finished, sealed in an envelope and taken by the Prime Minister himself, Nicholas Pasic, for delivery to the Austrian ambassador. Within an hour of its receipt, the personnel of the legation had boarded the train for the Austrian frontier and left Belgrade.

There followed a curious two-day intermission, Sunday and Monday, 26–27 July. Serbia mobilised its little army, Russia recalled the youngest reservists to the units in its western military districts, there were scenes of popular enthusiasm in Vienna over the government's rejection of the Serbian reply and similar scenes in German cities, including Berlin. On Sunday, however, the Kaiser was still at sea, while Poincaré and Viviani, the French Foreign Minister, aboard *La France*, did not receive a signal urging their immediate return until that night. Meanwhile there was much talk, reflective and anticipatory, rather than decisive or belligerent . . .

Austria-Hungary declared war on Serbia on Tuesday 28 July. It was Berchtold rather than Conrad who was now in a hurry. There had already been an exchange of fire between Serbian and Austrian troops—it was one-sided, an Austrian volley at Serbs who had strayed too near the Austrian border—but Berchtold chose to regard it as an act of war. War was now what he wanted on the terms he might have had during the days immediately following the murders, a straightforward offensive against Serbia uncomplicated by a wider conflict. The month's delay had threatened that simplicity, but he retained hopes that diplomacy would delay the taking of irretrievable decisions by others while he settled the Serbian score . . .

By the beginning of what was to prove the last week of peace, half the Russian army—though the half not stationed in the military districts adjoining Germany, those in Poland, White Russia and the Baltic provinces—was coming to a war footing. France had been informed and approved; indeed, Messimy, the Minister of War, and Joffre, the Chief of Staff, were pressing the Russians to achieve the highest possible state of readiness. The Russian generals at least needed little urging. Their responsibility as they saw it—all generals in all countries in July 1914 saw their responsibility in such terms—was to prepare for the worst if the worst came. The worst for them would be that, in seeking to deter Austria from making war in Serbia, their preparations provoked Germany into full-scale mobilisation. That would come about if their partial mobilisation, already in progress, prompted a full Austrian mobilisation which, they had good reason to believe, required a full German mobilisation also. On Tuesday 28 July, therefore, the Russian Chief of Staff, Janushkevich, with his quartermaster-general, chief of mobilisation and chief of trans-portation, agreed that the "Period Preparatory to War" must now be superseded by formal mobilisation announcements. Privately they accepted that general war could probably not be avoided: the sequence Russian partial mobilisation against Austria = Austrian general mobilisation = German general mobilisation = war stood stark before them . . .

The hour had come. That evening the posters announcing mobilisation went up in the streets of St. Petersburg and
of all cities in Russia. The reservists would begin reporting to
their depots next day, Friday 31 July. For reasons never properly
elucidated, what was necessary knowledge for every Russian
failed officially to reach London and Paris until late that
evening; the British ambassador was dilatory in telegraphing,
Paléologue's telegram was inexplicably delayed. The Germans
were not so ill-informed. They knew on Friday morning. At
10:20 a telegram arrived for Pourtaks, their ambassador in St.
Petersburg, "First day of mobilisation, 31 July." It was what
Moltke wanted to hear. He would now get the permission he
needed to take the military precautions he believed essential.
It was not what Bethmann Hollweg wanted to hear. He had
retained the hopes up to the moment of the telegram's arrival
that Austria could be brought directly to negotiate with Russia
and that Russia could be brought to accept the war against
Serbia as local and limited. Now he had to accept what seemed
inevitable. News of Austria's general mobilisation arrived half an
hour after noon. Germany proclaimed the "State of Danger of
War" half an hour after that.

The "State of Danger of War" was an internal measure
not entailing mobilisation. Nevertheless with Austria and
Russia mobilising, the Germans concluded that they must
mobilise also unless Russian general mobilisation was
reversed. An ultimatum to that effect was sent soon after
three o'clock on the afternoon of 31 July to St. Petersburg and
another to Paris . . .

The afternoon of 31 July thus brought to a crux the crisis which had begun thirty-four days earlier with the murders at Sarajevo. Its real duration had been much shorter than that. From the murders on 28 June to the conclusion of the Austrian judicial investigation and the confessions of the conspirators on 2 July was five days. It was in the period immediately following that the Austrians might have decided for unilateral action, and taken it without strong likelihood of provoking an intervention by the Serbs' protectors, the Russians. Instead, Austria had sought a German assurance of support, given on 5 July; elapsed time from the murders, eight days. There had then followed an intermission of nineteen days, while the Austrians waited for the French President to conclude his state visit on 23 July. The real inception of the crisis may thus be dated to the delivery of the Austrian "note with a time limit" (of forty-eight hours) on 24 July. It was on its expiry on Saturday 25 July, twenty-eight days from the murders, that the diplomatic confrontation was abruptly transformed into a war crisis . . .

It was the events of 31 July, therefore, the dissemination of the news of Russian general mobilisation, and the German ultimata to Russia and France, which made the issue one of peace or war. The day following, 1 August, the thirty-fifth since the murders, would bring Germany's mobilisation against Russia—thus making, in the words of the German ultimatum to France, "war inevitable"—unless Germany withdrew its ultimatum to Russia, which was incompatible with its status as a great power, or Russia accepted it, which was incompatible with such status also. German mobilisation would, under the terms of the Franco-Russian Convention of 1892, require both to mobilise and, if either were attacked by Germany, to go jointly to war against her. As the hours drew out on 31 July—the twelve demanded for a response from Russia, the eighteen demanded from France—only a hair's breadth kept the potential combatants apart. There was still a hope. The Russo-French Convention of 1892, strictly interpreted, required that Germany actually attack one country or the other before the two went to war against her. German mobilisation entailed only their mobilisation. Even a German declaration of war, unless followed by German military action, would not bring the treaty into force . . .

War hovered half a day away . . .

Yet the irrevocable did not yet seem done. The Tsar still hoped, on the strength of a telegram from the Kaiser begging him not to violate the German frontier, that war could be averted. The Kaiser, meanwhile, had fixed on the belief that the British would remain neutral if France were not attacked and was ordering Moltke to cancel the Schlieffen Plan and direct the army eastward. Moltke was aghast, explained that the paperwork would take a year, but was ordered to cancel the invasion of Luxembourg, which was the Schlieffen Plan's necessary preliminary. In London this Sunday 1 [2] August, the French ambassador, Paul Cambon, was thrown into despair by the British refusal to declare their position. Britain had, throughout the crisis, pursued the idea that, as so often before, direct talks between the involved parties would dissolve the difficulties. As a power apart, bound by treaties with none, it had concealed its intentions from all, including the French. Now the French demanded that the understanding between them and the British be given force. Would Britain declare outright its support for France and, if so, on what issue and when? The British themselves did not know. Throughout Saturday and Sunday 2 August, the cabinet debated its course of action . . .

Then, on 2 August, Germany delivered the last of its ultimata, this time to Belgium, demanding the use of its territory in operations against France and threatening to treat the country as an enemy if she resisted. The ultimatum was to expire in twenty-four hours, on Monday 3 August. It was the day Germany also decided, claiming violation of its own territory by French aircraft, to present France with a declaration of war. The expiry of the ultimatum to Belgium, which the British cabinet had finally resolved would constitute a cause for war, proved the irrevocable event. On Tuesday 4 August, Britain sent an ultimatum of its own, demanding the termination of German military operations against Belgium, which had already begun, to expire at midnight. No offer of termination in reply was received. At midnight, therefore, Britain, together with France and Russia, was at war with Germany.

The First World War had still not quite begun. The Austrians succeeded in delaying their declaration of war on Russia until 5 August and were still not at war with Britain and France a week later. Those two countries were driven to make up the Austrians' mind for them by announcing hostilities on 12 August. The Italians, Triple Alliance partners to Austria-Hungary and Germany, had stood on the strict terms of the treaty and declared their neutrality. The Serbs, cause of the crisis in the first place, had been forgotten. War was not to come to their little kingdom for another fourteen months.

CHAPTER TWO

CULTURE: AMERICA'S ENTRANCE INTO THE WAR

"The 'Lusitania'—And After"
From The Life and Letters of Walter H. Page
By Burton J. Hendrick
1923

Thanks to the urging of President Wilson, who reminded Americans to stay out of this "European war," the United States was still a neutral country in the middle of 1915. While concern for the nations involved was strong, so was the reluctance to become a part of their war. That sentiment began to change, however, when German submarines, referred to as U-boats, began sinking any ship they encountered. In October 1914, they sunk the British steamship Glitra. *Time to evacuate crew and passengers was allowed, but that amenity was quickly discarded. When the Germans sank Japan's* Tokomaru *and* Ikaria *without warning, the world started to turn against Germany for its brutality. The Germans did not appear to care.*

Different nations scrambled to come up with the technology to buffer these U-boat attacks. They invented nets to capture them underwater, as well as depth bombs that a merchant ship could shoot straight down if it detected a moving submarine beneath it. One of the most effective inventions was the hydrophone, an underwater microphone that could pick up the sounds of a U-boat's engine and the noise of the water being churned by its propeller. These inventions helped, but they were not enough to prevent more tragedies.

In May 1915, a U-boat torpedoed the British ship Lusitania, *and 1,198 people were killed or drowned. More than a hundred of them were Americans. The United States and President Wilson were outraged and demanded that Germany stop these attacks and respect the United States' neutrality on the seas. On the outside, Germany agreed. However, in August, the* Arabic *was sunk, and the next month, so was the* Hesperia. *Finally, in February 1917, the Germans sunk a U.S. Navy ship called the* Housatonic. *It was the final straw for President Wilson and for a country that had had enough of Germany's deceptions.*

———◻———

The news of the *Lusitania* was received at the American Embassy at four o'clock on the afternoon of May 7, 1915. At that time preparations were under way for a dinner in honour of Colonel and Mrs. House; the first *Lusitania* announcement declared that only the ship itself had been destroyed and that all the passengers and members of the crew had been saved; there was, therefore, no good reason for abandoning this dinner.

At about seven o'clock, the Ambassador came home; his manner showed that something extraordinary had taken place; there were no outward signs of emotion, but he was very serious. The first news, he now informed Mrs. Page, had been a mistake; more than one thousand men, women, and children had lost their lives, and more than one hundred of these were American citizens. It was too late to postpone the dinner but that affair was one of the most tragic in the social history of London. The Ambassador was constantly receiving bulletins from his Chancery, and these, as quickly as they were received, he read to his guests. His voice was quiet and subdued; there were no indications of excitement in his manner or in that of his friends, and hardly of suppressed emotion.

The atmosphere was rather that of dumb stupefaction. The news seemed to have dulled everyone's capacity for thought and even for feeling. If any one spoke, it was in whispers. Afterward, in the drawing room, this same mental state was the prevailing one; there was little denunciation of Germany and practically no discussion as to the consequences of the crime; everyone's thought was engrossed by the harrowing and unbelievable facts which the Ambassador was reading from the little yellow slips that were periodically brought in. An irresistible fascination evidently kept everybody in the room; the guests stayed late, eager for every new item. When they finally left, one after another, their manner was still abstracted and they said their good-nights in low voices. There were two reasons for this behaviour. The first was that the Ambassador and his guests had received the details of the greatest infamy which any supposedly civilized state had perpetrated since the massacre of Saint Bartholomew. The second was the conviction that the United States would at once declare war on Germany.

On this latter point several of the guests expressed their ideas and one of the most shocked and outspoken was Colonel House. For a month the President's personal representative had been discussing with British statesmen possible openings for mediation, but all his hopes in this direction now vanished. That President Wilson would act with the utmost energy Colonel House took for granted. This act, he evidently believed, left the United States no option. "We shall be at war with Germany within a month," he declared.

The feeling that prevailed in the Embassy this evening was the one that existed everywhere in London for several days. Emotionally the event acted like an anæsthetic. This was certainly the condition of all Americans associated with the American Embassy, especially Page himself. A day or two after the sinking the Ambassador went to Euston Station, at an early hour in the morning, to receive the American survivors. The hundred or more men and women who shambled from the train made a listless and bedraggled gathering. Their grotesque clothes, torn and unkempt—for practically none had had the opportunity of obtaining a change of dress—their expressionless faces, their lustreless eyes, their uncertain and bewildered walk, faintly reflected an experience such as comes to few people in this world. The most noticeable thing about these unfortunates was their lack of interest in their surroundings; everything had apparently been reduced to a blank; the fact that practically none made any reference to their ordeal, or could be induced to discuss it, was a matter of common talk in London. And something of this disposition now became noticeable in Page himself. He wrote his dispatches to Washington in an

abstracted mood; he went through his duties almost with the
detachment of a sleep-walker; like the *Lusitania* survivors, he
could not talk much at that time about the scenes that had
taken place off the coast of Ireland. Yet there were many indications that he was thinking about them, and his thoughts, as
his letters reveal, were concerned with more things than the
tragedy itself. He believed that his country was now face to
face with its destiny. What would Washington do?

Page had a characteristic way of thinking out his problems. He performed his routine work at the Chancery in the
daytime, but his really serious thinking he did in his own room
at night. The picture is still a vivid one in the recollection of
his family and his other intimates. Even at this time Page's
health was not good, yet he frequently spent the evening at his
office in Grosvenor Gardens, and when the long day's labours
were finished, he would walk rather wearily to his home at No.
6 Grosvenor Square. He would enter the house slowly—and his
walk became slower and more tired as the months went by—go
up to his room and cross to the fireplace, so apparently
wrapped up in his own thoughts that he hardly greeted members of his own family. A wood fire was kept burning for him,
winter and summer alike; Page would put on his dressing
gown, drop into a friendly chair, and sit there, doing nothing,
reading nothing, saying nothing—only thinking. Sometimes he
would stay for an hour; not infrequently he would remain till
two, three, or four o'clock in the morning; occasions were not
unknown when his almost motionless figure would be in this
same place at daybreak. He never slept through these nights,
and he never even dozed; he was wide awake, and his mind

was silently working upon the particular problem that was uppermost in his thoughts. He never rose until he had solved it or at least until he had decided upon a course of action. He would then get up abruptly, go to bed, and sleep like a child. The one thing that made it possible for a man of his delicate frame, racked as it was by anxiety and over work, to keep steadily at his task, was the wonderful gift which he possessed of sleeping.

Page had thought out many problems in this way. The tension caused by the sailing of the *Dacia*, in January, 1915, and the deftness with which the issue had been avoided by substituting a French for a British cruiser, has already been described. Page discovered this solution on one of these all-night self-communings. It was almost two o'clock in the morning that he rose, said to himself, "I've got it!" and then went contentedly to bed. And during the anxious months that followed the *Lusitania*, the *Arabic*, and those other outrages which have now taken their place in history, he spent night after night turning the matter over in his mind. But he found no way out of the humiliations presented by the policy of Washington.

"Here we are swung loose in time," he wrote to his son Arthur, a few days after the first *Lusitania* note had been sent to Germany, "nobody knows the day or the week or the month or the year—and we are caught on this island, with no chance of escape, while the vast slaughter goes on and seems just beginning, and the degradation of war goes on week by week; and we live in hope that the United States will come in, as the only chance to give us standing and influence when the reorganization of the world must begin.

(Beware of betraying the word 'hope'!) It has all passed far beyond anybody's power to describe. I simply go on day by day into unknown experiences and emotions, seeing nothing before me very clearly and remembering only dimly what lies behind. I can see only one proper thing: that all the world should fall to and hunt this wild beast down . . . "

The sensations of most Americans in London during this crisis are almost indescribable. Washington's failure promptly to meet the situation affected them with astonishment and humiliation. Colonel House was confident that war was impending, and for this reason he hurried his preparations to leave England; he wished to be in the United States, at the President's side, when the declaration was made. With this feeling about Mr. Wilson, Colonel House received a fearful shock a day or two after the *Lusitania* had gone down: while walking in Piccadilly, he caught a glimpse of one of the famous sandwich men, bearing a poster of an afternoon newspaper. This glaring broadside bore the following legend: "We are too proud to fight—Woodrow Wilson." The sight of that placard was Colonel House's first intimation that the President might not act vigorously. He made no attempt to conceal from Page and other important men at the American Embassy the shock which it had given him. Soon the whole of England was ringing with these six words; the newspapers were filled with stinging editorials and cartoons, and the music halls found in the Wilsonian phrase materials for their choicest jibes. Even in more serious quarters America was the subject of the most severe denunciation. No one felt these strictures more poignantly than President Wilson's closest confidant. A day or two before sailing home he came into the Embassy greatly depressed at the prevailing revulsion against the United States. "I feel," Colonel House said to Page, "as though I had been given a kick at every lamp post coming down Constitution Hill." A day or two afterward Colonel House sailed for America.

A Proclamation Issued to the American People By Woodrow Wilson April 15, 1917

Finally, it was apparent that the United States could no longer stay out of this ongoing war in Europe. After the sinking of the Housatonic, *Wilson had severed all diplomatic relations with Germany. A month later, a coded message from German foreign secretary Alfred Zimmerman to his ambassador stationed in Mexico forced the issue. British intelligence had intercepted and decoded it. When President Wilson saw its content, he knew the period of American neutrality was over. The Zimmerman telegram, as it became known, proposed a Germany-Mexico alliance against the United States. Sent in January 1917, it was published in newspapers across the world in March. The United States was shocked, and emotions ran high.*

On April 6, 1917, the United States made an official declaration of war. Nine days later, President Wilson made the following speech to the American people. It was a stirring speech and one that garnered deafening applause and cheers. Even though it went well, the president knew just what he was asking his country to do, and it saddened him. After the speech, he was reported to have said to his personal secretary, Joseph P. Tumulty, "Think what they were applauding! My message today was a message of death to our young men."

———□———

My Fellow Countrymen

The entrance of our own beloved country into the grim and terrible war for democracy and human rights which has shaken the world creates so many problems of national life and action which call for immediate consideration and settlement that I hope you will permit me to address to you a few words of earnest counsel and appeal with regard to them.

We are rapidly putting our navy upon an effective war footing and are about to create and equip a great army, but these are the simplest parts of the great task to which we have addressed ourselves.

There is not a single selfish element, so far as I can see, in the cause we are fighting for. We are fighting for what we believe and wish to be the rights of mankind and for the future peace and security of the world.

To do this great thing worthily and successfully we must devote ourselves to the service without regard to profit or material advantage and with an energy and intelligence that will rise to the level of the enterprise itself. We must realize to the full how great the task is and how many things, how many kinds and elements of capacity and service and self-sacrifice it involves.

These, then, are the things we must do, and do well, besides fighting—the things without which mere fighting would be fruitless.

We must supply abundant food for ourselves and for our armies and our seamen, not only, but also for a large part of the nations with whom we have now made common cause, in whose support and by whose sides we shall be fighting . . .

Soldiers Behind the Firing Line

The industrial forces of the country, men and women alike, will be a great national, a great international, service army—a notable and honoured host engaged in the service of the nation and the world, the efficient friends and saviours of free men everywhere.

Thousands—nay, hundreds of thousands—of men otherwise liable to military service will of right and of necessity be excused from that service and assigned to the fundamental, sustaining work of the fields and factories and mines, and they will be as much part of the great patriotic forces of the nation as the men under fire.

I take the liberty, therefore, of addressing this word to the farmers of the country and to all who work on the farms: The supreme need of our own nation and of the nations with which we are cooperating is an abundance of supplies, and especially of foodstuffs.

The importance of an adequate food supply, especially for the present years is superlative. Without abundant food, alike for the armies and the peoples now at war, the whole great enterprise upon which we have embarked will break down and fail.

The world's food reserves are low. Not only during the present emergency, but for some time after peace shall have come, both our own people and a large proportion of the people of Europe must rely upon the harvests in America.

Where the Fate of the War Rests

Upon the farmers of this country, therefore, in large measure rests the fate of the war and the fate of the nations. May the nation not count upon them to omit no step that will increase the production of their land or that will bring about the most effectual cooperation in the sale and distribution of their products?

The time is short. It is of the most imperative importance that everything possible be done, and done immediately, to make sure of large harvests.

I call upon young men and old alike and upon the able-bodied boys of the land to accept and act upon this duty—to turn in hosts to the farms and make certain that no pains and no labour is lacking in this great matter.

I particularly appeal to the farmers of the South to plant abundant foodstuffs, as well as cotton. They can show their patriotism in no better or more convincing way than by resisting the great temptation of the present price of cotton and helping, helping upon a great scale, to feed the nation and the peoples everywhere who are fighting for their liberties and for our own. The variety of their crops will be the visible measure of their comprehension of their national duty.

The Government of the United States and the governments of the several States stand ready to cooperate. They will do everything possible to assist farmers in securing an adequate supply of seed, an adequate force of labourers when they are most needed, at harvest time, and the means of expediting shipments of fertilizers and farm machinery, as well as of the crops themselves when harvested.

A Democracy's Chance to Make Good

The course of trade shall be as unhampered as it is possible to make it, and there shall be no unwarranted manipulation of the nation's food supply by those who handle it on its way to the consumer. This is our opportunity to demonstrate the efficiency of a great democracy, and we shall not fall short of it!

This let me say to the middlemen of every sort, whether they are handling our foodstuffs or our raw materials of manufacture or the products of our mills and factories: The eyes of the country will be especially upon you. This is your opportunity for signal service, efficient and disinterested.

The country expects you, as it expects all others, to forego unusual profits, to organize and expedite shipments of supplies of every kind, but especially of food, with an eye to the service you are rendering and in the spirit of those who enlist in the ranks, for their people, not for themselves.

I shall confidently expect you to deserve and win the confidence of people of every sort and station.

To the men who run the railways of the country, whether they be managers or operative employees, let me say that the railways are the arteries of the nation's life, and that upon them rests the immense responsibility of seeing to it that those arteries suffer no obstruction of any kind, no inefficiency or slackened power.

To the merchant let me suggest the motto, "Small profits and quick service," and to the shipbuilder the thought that the life of the war depends upon him. The food and the war supplies must be carried across the seas, no matter how many ships are sent to the bottom. The places of those that go down must be supplied, and supplied at once.

Statesmen and Armies Helpless Without Miners

To the miner let me say that he stands where the farmer does—the work of the world waits on him. If he slackens or fails, armies and statesmen are helpless. He also is enlisted in the great service army.

The manufacturer does not need to be told, I hope, that the nation looks to him to speed and perfect every process; and I want only to remind his employees that their service is absolutely indispensable and is counted on by every man who loves the country and its liberties.

Let me suggest, also, that every one who creates or cultivates a garden helps and helps greatly, to solve the problem of the feeding of the nations—and that every housewife who practices strict economy puts herself in the ranks of those who serve the nation. This is the time for America to correct her unpardonable fault of wastefulness and extravagance.

Let every man and every woman assume the duty of careful, provident use and expenditure as a public duty, as a dictate of patriotism which no one can now expect ever to be excused or forgiven for ignoring.

The Supreme Test Has Come

In the hope that this statement of the needs of the nation and of the world in this hour of supreme crisis may stimulate those to whom it comes and remind all who need reminder of the solemn duties of a time such as the world has never seen before, I beg that all editors and publishers everywhere will give as prominent publication and as wide circulation as possible to this appeal.

I venture to suggest, also, to all advertising agencies that they would perhaps render a very substantial and timely service to the country if they would give it wide-spread repetition.

And I hope that clergymen will not think the theme of it an unworthy or inappropriate subject of comment and homily from their pulpits.

The supreme test of the nation has come. We must all speak, act, and serve together!

Woodrow Wilson

The White House

A Speech to Congress by Senator Robert "Fightin' Bob" La Follette
October 6, 1917

On the surface, it appeared that the entire nation was behind President Wilson's decision to finally enter into the war. However, as Lincoln once said, "You can't please all of the people all of the time," and this was certainly true when the country's neutrality over World War I ended. A small group of

*men in Congress were decidedly against joining the war and
had voted against it. Although their dissension was lost in
America's rush of loud and eager patriotism, they had a
spokesperson to make sure it was not completely silenced. He
was a senator from Wisconsin, and his name was Robert La
Follette, known to friends and opponents alike as Fightin' Bob.
La Follette had already established a reputation for being outspoken about his opinions and stances on various issues, and
the United States' involvement in the war was no exception.*

*La Follette shared his thoughts with everyone in the
Senate on October 6, 1917. He passionately defended every
American's right to free speech, including being able to state
they were against the war and not be criticized, labeled, or
harassed for doing so. His words echoed the thoughts of
many and reminded the country that the decision to go to war
is a complex, solemn, and far-reaching decision.*

————□————

Mr. President:

I rise to a question of personal privilege. I have no inten-
tion of taking the time of the Senate with a review of the
events which led to our entrance into the war except in so far
as they bear upon the question of personal privilege to which I
am addressing myself.

Six Members of the Senate and fifty Members of the
House voted against the declaration of war. Immediately
there was let loose upon those Senators and Representatives
a flood of invective and abuse from newspapers and individuals
who had been clamoring for war, unequaled, I believe in the
history of civilized society.

Prior to the declaration of war every man who had ventured to oppose our entrance into it had been condemned as a coward or worse, and even the President had by no means been immune from these attacks.

Since the declaration of war the triumphant war press has pursued those Senators and Representatives who voted against war with malicious falsehood and recklessly libelous attacks, going to the extreme limit of charging them with treason against their country.

This campaign of libel and character assassination directed against the Members of Congress who opposed our entrance into the war has been continued down to the present hour, and I have upon my desk newspaper clippings, some of them libels upon me alone, some directed as well against other Senators who voted in opposition to the declaration of war. One of these newspaper reports most widely circulated represents a Federal judge in the state of Texas as saying, in a charge to a grand jury—I read the article as it appeared in the newspaper and the headline with which it is introduced:

[La Follette picks up newspaper and reads aloud.]

District Judge Would Like to Take Shot at Traitors in Congress

(A.P.) HOUSTON, TEXAS, OCT 1, Judge Waller T. Burns of the United States district court, in charging a Federal grand jury at the beginning of the October term today, after calling by name Senators Stone of Missouri, Hardwick of Georgia, Vardaman of Mississippi, Gronna of North Dakota, Gore of

Oklahoma, and La Follette of Wisconsin, said: "If I
had a wish, I would wish that you men had jurisdiction to return bills of indictment against these men.
They ought to be tried promptly and fairly, and I
believe this court could administer the law fairly;
but I have a conviction, as strong as life, that this
country should stand them up against an adobe
wall tomorrow and give them what they deserve. If
any man deserves death, it is a traitor. I wish that I
could pay for the ammunition. I would like to
attend the execution, and if I were in the firing
squad I would not want to be the marksman who
had the blank shell." . . .

If this newspaper clipping were a single or exceptional
instance of lawless defamation, I should not trouble the
Senate with a reference to it. But, Mr. President, it is not.

In this mass of newspaper clippings which I have here
upon my desk, and which I shall not trouble the Senate to read
unless it is desired, I find other Senators, as well as myself,
accused of the highest crimes of which any man can be
guilty—treason and disloyalty—and, sir, accused not only with
no evidence to support the accusation, but without the suggestion that such evidence anywhere exists. It is not claimed that
Senators who opposed the declaration of war have since that
time acted with any concerted purpose either regarding war
measures or any others. They have voted according to their
individual opinions, have often been opposed to each other on
bills which have come before the Senate since the declaration

of war, and, according to my recollection, have never all voted together since that time upon any single proposition upon which the Senate has been divided.

I am aware, Mr. President, that in pursuance of this campaign of vilification and attempted intimidation, requests from various individuals and certain organizations have been submitted to the Senate for my expulsion from this body, and that such requests have been referred to and considered by one of the committees of the Senate.

If I alone had been made the victim of these attacks, I should not take one moment of the Senate's time for their consideration, and I believe that other Senators who have been unjustly and unfairly assailed, as I have been, hold the same attitude upon this that I do. Neither the clamor of the mob nor the voice of power will ever turn me by the breadth of a hair from the course I mark out for myself, guided by such knowledge as I can obtain and controlled and directed by a solemn conviction of right and duty.

But, sir, it is not alone Members of Congress that the war party in this country has sought to intimidate. The mandate seems to have gone forth to the sovereign people of this country that they must be silent while those things are being done by their Government which most vitally concern their well-being, their happiness, and their lives. Today and for weeks past honest and law-abiding citizens of this country are being terrorized and outraged in their rights by those sworn to uphold the laws and protect the rights of the people. I have in my possession numerous affidavits establishing the fact that people are being unlawfully arrested, thrown into jail, held incommunicado for days, only to be eventually discharged without ever having been taken into court, because they have committed no crime. Private residences are being invaded, loyal citizens of undoubted integrity and probity arrested, cross-examined, and the most sacred constitutional rights guaranteed to every American citizen are being violated.

It appears to be the purpose of those conducting this campaign to throw the country into a state of terror, to coerce public opinion, to stifle criticism, and suppress discussion of the great issues involved in this war.

I think all men recognize that in time of war the citizen must surrender some rights for the common good which he is entitled to enjoy in time of peace. But sir, the right to control their own Government according to constitutional forms is not one of the rights that the citizens of this country are called upon to surrender in time of war.

Rather in time of war the citizen must be more alert to the preservation of his right to control his Government. He must be most watchful of the encroachment of the military upon the civil power. He must beware of those precedents in support of arbitrary action by administration officials which, excused on the plea of necessity in war time, become the fixed rule when the necessity has passed and normal conditions have been restored.

More than all, the citizen and his representative in Congress in time of war must maintain his right of free speech. More than in times of peace it is necessary that the channels for free public discussion of governmental policies shall be open and unclogged. I believe, Mr. President, that I am now touching upon the most important question in this country today—and that is the right of the citizens of this country and their representatives in Congress to discuss in an orderly way frankly and publicly and without fear, from the platform and through the press, every important phase of this war; its causes, and manner in which it should be conducted, and the terms upon which peace should be made. The belief which is becoming widespread in this land that this most fundamental right is being denied to the citizens of this country is a fact, the tremendous significance of which those in authority have not yet begun to appreciate. I am contending, Mr. President, for the great fundamental right of the sovereign people of this country to make their voice heard and have that voice heeded upon the great questions arising out of this war, including not only how the war shall be prosecuted but the conditions upon which it may be terminated with a due regard for the rights and the honor of this Nation and the interests of humanity.

I am contending for this right because the exercise of it is necessary to the welfare, to the existence, of this Government, to the successful conduct of this war, and to a peace which shall be enduring for the best interest of this country.

Suppose success attends the attempt to stifle all discussion of the issues of this war, all discussions of the terms upon which it should be concluded, all discussion of the objects and purposes to be accomplished by it, and concede the demand of the war-mad press and war extremists that they monopolize the right of public utterance upon these questions unchallenged, what think you would be the consequences to this country not only during the war but after the war?

It is no answer to say that when the war is over the citizen may once more resume his rights and feel some security in his liberty and his person. As I have already tried to point out, now is precisely the time when the country needs the counsel of all its citizens. In time of war even more than in time of peace, whether citizens happen to agree with the ruling administration or not, these precious fundamental personal rights— free speech, free press, and right of assemblage so explicitly and emphatically guaranteed by the Constitution should be maintained inviolable. There is no rebellion in the land, no martial law, no courts are closed, no legal processes suspended, and there is no threat even of invasion.

But more than this, if every preparation for war can be made the excuse for destroying free speech and a free press and the right of the people to assemble together for peaceful discussion, then we may well despair of ever again finding ourselves for a long period in a state of peace . . . The destruction of rights now occurring will be pointed to them as precedents for a still further invasion of the rights of the citizen . . .

Mr. President, our Government, above all others, is founded on the right of the people freely to discuss all matters pertaining to their Government, in war not less than in peace. It is true, sir, that Members of the House of Representatives are elected for two years, the President for four years, and the Members of the Senate for six years, and during their temporary official terms these officers constitute what is called the Government. But back of them always is the controlling sovereign power of the people, and when the people can make their will known, the faithful officer will obey that will. Though the right of the people to express their will by ballot is suspended during the term of office of the elected official, nevertheless the duty of the official to obey the popular will continues throughout his entire term of office. How can that popular will express itself between elections except by meetings, by speeches, by publications, by petitions, and by addresses to the representatives of the people? Any man who seeks to set a limit upon those rights, whether in war or peace, aims a blow at the most vital part of our Government. And then as the time for election approaches and the official is called to account for his stewardship—not a day, not a week, not a month, before the election, but a year or more before it, if the people choose—they must have the right to the freest possible discussion of every question upon which their representative has acted, of the merits of every measure he has supported or opposed, of every vote he has cast and every speech that he has made. And before this great fundamental right every other must, if necessary, give way, for in no other manner can representative government be preserved.

"A Nation at War"
From Yanks
By John S. Eisenhower
2001

Getting Americans to publicly support the United States' involvement in the war was not terribly difficult. Although there would always be those who did not agree with the action, the sinking of the Lusitania *and the* Housatonic *had already soured the people's opinions of the Central powers. When the*

Zimmerman telegram was published in papers across the country, those feelings intensified. John S. Eisenhower, son of Dwight D. Eisenhower, and retired officer turned military historian, gives an account of the American attitude on the eve of its entrance into the Great War.

As the nation moved closer and closer to a formal declaration of war, emotions deepened. Although the president continued to remind the world that the United States was still neutral, complex military preparations were still under way. Republicans like former president Theodore Roosevelt and Henry Cabot Lodge supported these steps, and their comments helped fuel the fire of Americans' anger. An attitude of intolerance and bigotry began to build, and patriotism sometimes went so far as to turn into obsession. This led, in some instances, to a true hatred of anything German—from innocent immigrants to beer.

———□———

When war was declared, active public support was wide but not universal. Few citizens contested the action in itself; resentment of German arrogance and ruthlessness had seen to that. But pockets of resistance still survived; for example, Senator James K. Vardaman, a Mississippi Democrat, had attempted to prevent the passage of the war declaration practically up to the last minute. Vardaman was a known Southern isolationist, and he did not represent a very large segment of the population, but enough people held similar viewpoints as to constitute a cause for concern. No American territory had been attacked to enrage the public, as would be the case with the Japanese raid on Pearl Harbor a quarter century later. In 1917 the general attitude of mere acceptance had to be transformed to one of zeal.

To mobilize public support, the President called on an intense man named George Creel, who had been an avid and visible supporter of Wilson's reelection campaign of 1916. Creel did not appear to be a man Wilson would prefer to associate with. True, both were native Virginians, but Wilson's family had spent the Civil War in relative safety and comfort in Augusta, Georgia, whereas Creel's people had been so impoverished that they pulled up stakes and migrated to Missouri just to eke out an existence. Creel, unlike Wilson, had been raised in a hard luck, street-smart world; his background of privation had made him an aggressive challenger of established society.

Creel was a man of action. He had pursued a varied career as a newspaper reporter, politician, professional boxer, and even police commissioner, always driven by a fiery intensity. As a newspaper man he had proudly lived up to the label of "muckraker." In recent years he had been engaged in attacking the Pendergast political machine in Kansas City; another target of his pen was the prevalence of cruel and abusive child labor. Creel had come to view the academic, lofty Wilson as a fellow reformer. It was on that basis that Creel had published his supportive campaign tract, *Wilson and the Issues*. Wilson was grateful, and when the time came to create the Committee on Public Information on April 13, 1917, he turned to this firebrand crusader as its chairman.

Creel lived up to all of Wilson's expectations. He set up an office on Jackson Square, across Pennsylvania Avenue from the White House, and there he began recruiting a group of journalists dedicated to spreading the word of the war's righteousness across the land. The committee's Division of News distributed more than six thousand press releases in the course of the war, and Creel later claimed that more than twenty thousand newspaper columns were derived from material issued in Committee on Public Information handouts. He enlisted the help of prominent motion picture personalities Mary Pickford, Douglas Fairbanks, and Charles Chaplin among them. An appearance by those three luminaries to sell Liberty Bonds on Wall Street brought a crowd of thirty thousand people. He organized a stable of cheerleaders that called themselves the Four Minute Men, who traveled the country giving short pep talks at rallies and in theaters. Creel even called on the great explorer Roald Amundsen to spread the word . . .

As might be expected, Creel offended some people, especially sober-minded citizens. Charges of censorship were leveled against him in some quarters. A zealot in promoting his product, Creel refused to tolerate any criticism toward the cause; since he dispensed the news, he had much power to control what the public learned. Nevertheless, Creel played a major role in changing the minds of people who for three years had observed strict neutrality in the war. In a remarkably short time his efforts completely reversed their reluctance.

George Creel's role in marshaling public support, while well-nigh indispensable, would have been meaningless if the enthusiastic men and women he was inspiring could not be organized into a cohesive war effort. Since President Wilson showed little personal interest in military matters, that task fell to an unusual degree on the shoulders of Secretary of War Newton Baker . . .

Baker was an ideal man for the job. He had been in his position about a year when the United States entered the war, and before coming to Washington he had been a successful lawyer, a solicitor of the city of Cleveland, and later an extremely effective mayor of the same city. He was devoted to Woodrow Wilson and had been Wilson's avid supporter in the presidential election in 1912. The pacifism he shared with the President was mitigated by his advocacy of military preparedness. Above all, Baker had earned a reputation for an ability to work with others.

He did not look the part of the man of Mars. Only forty-six years old, small of stature, and unpretentious, his prominent eyeglasses gave him the appearance of a schoolmaster. But by the time war came, this quiet little man had proved to be quite capable of directing armies and headstrong commanders.

His relations with Chief of Staff Hugh Scott were cordial. He respected the old Indian fighter and early in the partnership had allowed Scott to play the role of a tutor. But Scott and the other generals who served under Baker had learned early that when the Secretary said no, that was exactly what he meant.

He also worked well with Secretary of the Navy Josephus Daniels. Daniels went so far, in fact, as to describe the two of them as "yoke fellows," a relationship that Daniels somewhat hyperbolically called "the 'perfect working together of the Army and the Navy' which made them invincible in the World War."

Baker's executive ability would be taxed in the months ahead, because the War Department had neither an adequate General Staff nor an effective chief of staff to head it. The men assigned to the General Staff were competent officers, thanks to the Army's excellent school system, but they were far too few. The traditional American fear of undue military influence in government had caused the Congress to limit the General Staff Corps to a paltry fifty-five officers, of whom only twenty-one could be stationed in Washington.

General Scott was a fine old officer, but he was only months away from the mandatory retirement age of sixty-four. Moreover, he hated office work. His shortcomings were partially offset by his deputy chief of staff, Tasker Bliss, who was a meticulous man, at home behind a desk. Bliss was a scholar, who had studied European military systems firsthand, and who earned Baker's admiration for his "habit of deliberate and consecutive thinking, his mind a comprehensive card index." Some said that Bliss spent too much time on trivia and lacked the ruthlessness necessary in a strong chief. But for the moment Baker had nobody to replace these two old soldiers with, so his own role took on added importance.

Much had happened during Baker's first year as Secretary of War. Soon after his arrival in early 1916, the public began to appreciate the need for an expanded, modernized army, and on May 20 Congress passed the National Defense Act of 1916, which provided for the authorized strength of the Regular Army to be raised to a level of 175,000 men, a goal to be reached at the end of five years. The act was motivated, however, by concern over relations with Mexico, not potential war with Germany. Among other shortcomings, it provided for a very limited expansion, to only 286,000 men, even in time of war. Of greater significance for the future was the emphasis it placed on the Army's reserve component, the National Guard, for which it authorized a ceiling of 400,000 men.

When war came nearly a year later, both Wilson and the Congress realized that the National Defense Act of 1916 could never provide even the 500,000 men the United States originally expected to send to Europe. A new bill was necessary, and the terms of that bill would determine the very nature of the army that was to be built.

The vast size of the proposed new army dictated that, as in previous American wars, it would consist largely of citizen-soldiers, men brought in from civil life and trained under the supervision of the Regulars. During the year that the previous act had been in effect, the total number of men in uniform came to 130,000 Regulars and about 70,000 National Guardsmen. Assuming that a total of a million men were needed, from what sources would the additional 800,000 men come? Would the nation have to implement a draft or could it raise that large number of troops solely from volunteers? Would the newly organized divisions be called Regular, National Guard, or something else? . . .

One man felt no ambivalence on the subject. From the start, Chief of Staff Hugh Scott would consider no solution whatever except for a national draft. He shared his views forcibly with Baker, who agreed. Baker then presented that recommendation to president Wilson, carefully presenting all sides of the debate. Some people, he advised, would object to a draft on constitutional grounds. Others remembered the bitter experiences the Union had undergone during the American Civil War, only fifty years earlier. After some discussion, Wilson and Baker made a courageous decision in favor of a draft, and the bulk of the American people supported it.

Baker and Wilson early came to one important conclusion. It was essential, they realized, that the American citizenry should be made to feel that the draft was theirs, not something imposed by an autocratic military. To accomplish that end, they directed that the inductees would be selected by draft boards made up of local citizens, appointed by the various governors throughout the country. To popularize the process, the bill cast the board members themselves in the position of draftees. Citizens so serving were not to be paid, and any attempt to avoid such onerous duty would be labeled a misdemeanor.

As might be expected, some resistance met the draft bill in Congress. Its progress was further hampered by the followers of Theodore Roosevelt, who introduced what became known as the Roosevelt Amendment, which held approval of Wilson's draft proposal hostage to a provision authorizing the former president to organize a division of volunteers . . .

The Selective Service Act was passed on May 19, 1917, mobilizing the manpower of the nation. It provided for the first registration of citizens between twenty-one and thirty-one to be held on June 5. In the course of the war, two more registrations would finally increase the range of ages from eighteen to forty-five inclusive. An impressive 24 million men were eventually registered, of which 2.8 million were actually inducted into service at one time or another. The draftees would soon be as fully accepted in the military as the Regulars, Guardsmen, and volunteers—and their desertion rate would be the lowest of those in any category.

On the morning of July 20, 1917, Secretary of War Baker stood blindfolded in his office, the cameras of the press whirring. He was to draw the first number in the lottery to determine who should be the first men called to active duty. Baker was to be followed by Senator George E. Chamberlain, of Oregon, chairman of the Senate Committee on Military Affairs. Many dignitaries participated. The last drawings were made by Acting Chief of Staff Tasker Bliss and General Enoch Crowder, whose office had written the draft act and who, now designated as Provost Marshal General, would actually conduct the draft.

Baker reached into a glass jar that contained 10,500 registration numbers written on slips of paper. He took hold of one and read it out: Number 258. Any man holding that number would immediately report to the draft board.

America's full manpower was now committed to the cause. The first men had been selected to create the National Army of the American Expeditionary Force.

CHAPTER THREE

INDIVIDUALS, GROUPS, AND INSTITUTIONS: THE WAR'S MEDIA AND PROPAGANDA MACHINE

An Open Letter Published in American Newspapers by Leading German Citizens
Issued by an Imposing Committee of Leading German Statesmen, Scholars, Bankers, and Merchants, Including Prince von Bulow, Marshal von der Goltz, Matthias Erzerberger, Herr Ballin, Count von Reventlow, and the Head of the Imperial Bank August 1914

Two of the weapons used in World War I did not shoot bullets or throw bombs; they did not require metal and moving parts. This did not make them any less lethal, however. These weapons were censorship and propaganda. Censorship was used to suppress information, such as reports on wounded and dead soldiers, to the public. What happened on the fronts had to be approved by military commanders before being released to the public.

Both sides flagrantly used propaganda, or information deliberately slanted to support one point of view over another. One country's actions were glorified; the enemy's actions were downplayed or skewed. Rumors flew in each direction;

*most of them intended to intimidate the other side. Leaflets
were dropped by airplanes over the endless miles of trenches
at the western front. They informed the enemy that doom
was inevitable and that they were the losers. Propaganda
even eventually made it to the theater in silent pictures such
as Charlie Chaplin's* Shoulder Arms *and Britain's* Battle of
the Somme.

———□———

Listen, All Ye People!

Try to realize, every one of you, what we are going
through! Only a few weeks ago all of us were peacefully following our several vocations. The peasant was gathering in
this summer's plentiful crop, the factory hand was working
with accustomed vigour.

Not one human being among us dreamed of war. We
are a nation that wishes to lead a quiet and industrious life.
This need hardly be stated to you Americans. You, of all
others, know the temper of the German who lives within
your gates.

Our love of peace is so strong that it is not regarded by
us in the light of a virtue, we simply know it to be an inborn
and integral portion of ourselves. Since the foundation of the
German Empire in the year 1871, we, living in the centre of
Europe, have given an example of tranquillity and peace,
never once seeking to profit by any momentary difficulties of
our neighbours.

Our commercial extension, our financial rise in the
world, are far removed from any love of adventure, they are
the fruit of painstaking and plodding labour.

We are not credited with this temper, because we are insufficiently known. Our situation and our way of thinking are not easily grasped.

Every one is aware that we have produced great philosophers and poets, we have preached the gospel of humanity with impassioned zeal. America fully appreciates Goethe and Kant, looks upon them as corner-stones of elevated culture. Do you really believe that we have changed our natures, that our souls can be satisfied with military drill and servile obedience?

We are soldiers because we have to be soldiers, because otherwise Germany and German civilization would be swept away from the face of the earth. It has cost us long and weary struggles to attain our independence, and we know full well that, in order to preserve it, we must not content ourselves with building schools and factories, we must look to our garrisons and forts.

We and all our soldiers have remained, however, the same lovers of music and lovers of exalted thought. We have retained our old devotion to all peaceable sciences and arts; as all the world knows, we work in the foremost rank of all those who strive to advance the exchange of commodities, who further useful, technical knowledge.

But we have been forced to become a nation of soldiers, in order to be free. And we are bound to follow our Kaiser, because he symbolizes and represents the unity of our nation. To-day, knowing no distinction of party, no difference of opinion, we rally around him, willing to shed the last drop of our blood.

For though it takes a great deal to rouse us Germans, when once aroused, our feelings run deep and strong. Every one is filled with this passion, with the soldier's ardour. But when the waters of the deluge shall have subsided, gladly will we return to the plow and to the anvil.

It deeply distresses us to see two highly civilized nations, England and France, joining the onslaught of autocratic Russia. That this could happen, will remain one of the anomalies of history. It is not our fault: we firmly believed in the desirability of the great nations working together, we peaceably came to terms with France and England in sundry difficult African questions.

There was no cause for war between Western Europe and us, no reason why Western Europe should feel itself constrained to further the power of the Czar.

The Czar, as an individual, is most certainly not the instigator of the unspeakable horrors that are now inundating Europe. But he bears before God and Posterity the responsibility of having allowed himself to be terrorized by an unscrupulous military clique.

Ever since the weight of the crown has pressed upon him, [he] has been the tool of others. He did not desire the brutalities in Finland, he did not approve of the iniquities of the Jewish Pogroms, but his hand was too weak to stop the fury of the reactionary party.

Why would he not permit Austria to pacify her southern frontier? It was inconceivable that Austria should calmly see her heir apparent murdered. How could she?

All the nationalities under her rule realized the impossibility of tamely allowing Serbia's only too evident and successful intrigues to be carried on under her very eyes.

The Austrians could not allow their venerable and sorely stricken monarch to be wounded and insulted any longer. This reasonable and honourable sentiment on the part of Austria has caused Russia to put itself forward as the patron of Serbia, as the enemy of European thought and civilization.

Russia has an important mission to fulfill in its own country and in Asia. It would do better in its own interest to leave the rest of the world in peace. But the die is cast, and all nations must decide whether they wish to further us by sentiments and by deeds, or the government of the Czar.

This is the real significance of this appalling struggle, all the rest is immaterial. Russia's attitude alone has forced us to go to war with France and with their great ally.

The German nation is serious and conscientious. Never would a German Government dare to contemplate a war for the sake of dynastic interest, or for the sake of glory. This would be against the entire bent of our character.

Firmly believing in the justice of our cause, all parties, the conservatives and the clericals, the liberals and the socialists, have joined hands. All disputes are forgotten, one duty exists for all, the duty of defending our country and vanquishing the enemy.

Will not this calm, self-reliant and unanimous readiness to sacrifice all, to die or to win, appeal to other nations and force them to understand our real character and the situation in which we are placed?

The war has severed us from the rest of the world, all our cable communications are destroyed. But the winds will carry the mighty voice of justice even across the ocean. We trust in God, we have confidence in the judgment of right-minded men. And through the roar of battle, we call to you all. Do not believe the mischievous lies that our enemies are spreading about!

We do not know if victory will be ours, the Lord alone knows. We have not chosen our path, we must continue doing our duty, even to the very end. We bear the misery of war, the death of our sons, believing in Germany, believing in duty.

And we know that Germany cannot be wiped from the face of the earth.

"Mutiny"
From The Great War and the Shaping of the 20th Century
By Jay Winter and Blaine Baggett
1996

In March 1917, rioting in Russia turned into a revolution. The czar stepped down from power, and a provisional government was set up. A group of 2,500 workers and military calling themselves the Petrograd Soviet Workers and Soldiers' Deputies immediately challenged this new system. While the provisional government voted to continue its role in the war, the Soviets did not agree. Each side was ordering the people to obey their rules as they fought for control of the nation.

The Soviets began to gather around the leadership of a man called Vladimir Ilyich Lenin. He called his followers Bolsheviks, which means majority. He referred to the others, those who did not believe his philosophies, as the Mensheviks, which means minority. Ironically, in number, the two groups were precisely the opposite. In November 1917, Lenin and his assistant, Leon Trotsky, led the Bolsheviks into a second revolution. They toppled the provisional government and turned Russia into a Communist state. In doing so, they agreed to make peace with Germany, and not long after, they began fighting on the side of the Central powers instead of the Allies. Historians Winter and Baggett examine here the people and timeline that lead to a major turning point in the war.

———□———

By 1917 the [Russian] Army was stretched to its limits, but still contained elements prepared to go on.

One was highly unusual. It was a women's battalion, "the battalion of death," led by Maria Botchkareva who was known to her soldiers as Yashka. Illiterate, married at the age of fifteen, abused by her first husband, exiled to Siberia with her second, she escaped from this harsh life into the Army. Her decision to join up was greeted with derision, but she sent a petition to the Tsar begging for the right to serve, and her appeal was approved.

In later years Yashka recounted her initiation—inconceivable outside of war—into this masculine world, and much of the abuse with which she had to contend to realize her dream. Some of her reminiscences were fanciful, but her career was not. She earned the respect of her comrades by sharing their hardships and by bringing wounded men back from No Man's Land. She suffered from frostbite and was wounded several times, once by shrapnel which temporarily paralyzed her.

Back at the front in 1917, she was stupefied by news of revolution. She recalled being astonished by the proclamation of "Freedom, Equality and Brotherhood" for all, and at the prospect of land for the landless. She welcomed the chance to swear allegiance to the new government and "drive the Germans out of Free Russia, before returning home to divide up the land."

Yashka believed in carrying on the war no matter what the cost. When the men in her unit decided enough was enough, Yashka went to Petrograd [St. Petersburg] to find another way of fighting. Her version of events is that she approached the former President of the Duma [Parliament], Rodzianko, with the idea of forming "a Women's Battalion of Death." Speaking to a group of soldiers' delegates: "'You have heard of what I have done and endured as a soldier,' I said, rising to my feet and turning to the audience. 'Now, how would it do to organize three hundred women like myself to serve as an example to the army and lead the men into battle?'" And this is precisely what she did. Her hope was "not to imitate the demoralized army," rather to restore discipline and duty. But, as she saw at the front, the rot had already set in; few units had the heart to carry on.

Yashka typified those who wanted to go on. So did Alexander Kerensky, who in June 1917 became the key figure in the Provisional Government. He ordered the Army to launch a new offensive in early July. The Germans counter-attacked. The Russian Army disintegrated.

The Battalion of Death—among other units—went forward, but to no avail. The Army was a broken reed. Yashka was knocked unconscious and taken to hospital with "shell shock." When she recovered, she found chaos in the Army. According to her memoirs, she had meetings with Kerensky and General Korniov, Commander of the Russian Army on the Southern Front, both of whom believed in restoring order through force. Their attempt to do so only produced a further loss of support for the Provisional Government. No one could reverse the tide taking Russia out of the war . . .

Leon Trotsky was one of them. In 1914 Leon Trotsky was a thirty-five-year-old revolutionary, more moderate than Lenin, a leader of the Revolution of 1905, on the Menshevik (moderate majority) wing of the Russian Social Democratic or RSD Party. He was a man of immense intellectual and oratorical power, and aware of his gifts. "He loved the workers and loved his comrades," wrote one colleague, "because in them he loved himself."

Like most other revolutionaries he was shocked at the collapse of international solidarity among workers, but he predicted correctly that in Russia the mass support for war of 1914 was merely a facade. In 1914–15 he was on the move, evading arrest as a subversive or undesirable alien agitator in a number of countries. This was the fate of most of the leaders of the Revolution of 1917. Many found a haven in Switzerland. There Lenin lived, after spending a short time in an Austrian jail in Galicia.

In September 1915, in the Swiss hamlet of Zimmerwald, Trotsky joined Lenin and Rosa Luxemburg (recently released from prison) in the first attempt to revive international socialism. At this time Trotsky was not a political ally of Lenin—he only joined the Bolsheviks, the radical minority of the RSD, two years later, in the midst of the Revolution.

In 1916 he was working as a military correspondent in Paris until in September his newspaper was banned and he was expelled from France. He crossed the Spanish border, was arrested, but after a delay was released to further exile in New York where he arrived in January 1917. There he edited another revolutionary newspaper, and according to legend worked on a film set in the Bronx.

The news of the uprising electrified him, on account of its meaning both for Russia and for the rest of the world. "In all the belligerent countries the lack of bread is the most immediate, the most acute reason for dissatisfaction and indignation among the masses," he wrote. "All the insanity of the war is revealed to them from this angle; it is impossible to produce the necessities of life because one has to produce instruments of death." Stirring words from New York, but to light the spark to set the world on fire he and all the other exiles had to return to Russia. This was no easy matter. After the February Revolution, his friends purchased a ticket to get him back to Russia. He left on 27 March, but six days later, en route, he was arrested by the British at Halifax, Nova Scotia— the remit of British Intelligence was broadly interpreted—and spent another period in jail. After further delay he was freed, and reached Petrograd on 17 May 1917.

Lenin had arrived at the Finland Station in Petrograd one month before. He had travelled across Germany in a sealed train generously provided by the German authorities, who were happy to help in subverting the new regime. Lenin immediately called for the overthrow of the Provisional Government and an end to the war.

Military Collapse and Political Upheaval

Subversion was unnecessary. Lenin and Trotsky did not make the revolution; they merely presided over a set of events arising from the Provisional Government's disastrous decision to go on with the war. By the summer of 1917, the population had simply had enough. Similar tensions existed in the West, but people there accepted hardship because it followed the consent of the governed . . .

Consent was precisely what was lacking when the Kerensky government ordered a new offensive in early July 1917. Gestures, like the deployment of the Women's Battalion of Death, were futile. As Trotsky put it, the Army had voted with their feet against the war.

It was in this atmosphere that units in Petrograd, including a few members of the Bolshevik Military Organization, were ordered to the front. Outraged, they took to the streets in armed demonstrations on 4 July to demand the overthrow of the Provisional Government. The uprising lasted two days, and was suppressed by loyal troops still backing the government . . .

Lenin and other leading Bolsheviks were forced into hiding. To Trotsky, the July days were the moment when the revolutionaries flexed their muscles. They had to retreat and regroup, but only to await the right moment to seize power. He himself was arrested on 23 July, but, like a latter-day Mafioso, still directed events from his prison cell. Only then, in August 1917, did he finally join the Central Committee of the Bolshevik Party.

When counter-revolutionary troops under General Kornilov threatened to overthrow the Provisional Government, some sailors visited Trotsky in prison to ask his advice: "Should they defend the Winter Palace or take it by assault? I advised them to put off the squaring of their account with Kerensky until they had finished Korniov. 'What's ours will not escape us.'"

"What's ours will not escape us": this phrase echoed through the vast reaches of the Russian Empire. From April 1917, thousands of peasants seized land in increasing numbers. First under the cloak of legality, then by force, the face of peasant Russia was transformed. This movement was applauded by the Bolsheviks, suddenly the champions of private property. Their position was realistic to some and cynical to others: they simply cheered on what could not be turned aside. The longer the conflict dragged on, the more Bolshevik support increased. As Trotsky put it: "Every soldier who expressed a little more boldly than the rest what they were all feeling, was so persistently shouted at from above as a Bolshevik that he was obliged in the long run to believe it. From peace and land the soldiers' thoughts began to pass over to the question of power."

The Seizure of Power

The partnership of Lenin and Trotsky—two men who treated each other with both respect and suspicion—is the key to the Russian Revolution. Lenin the political direction; Trotsky the military force to achieve it . . .

The insurrection itself was Trotsky's design. He personally directed operations from the Smolny Institute. A thousand tasks needed coordination: a detachment of troops had to secure the printing presses of the Bolshevik Party, which had been shut down by the Provisional Government; another squad had to evict military academy students who were blocking the telephone exchange; and so on. On 24 October, the tension rose . . .

During those hours, Red Guards, with the help of some regular army units, gained control of key factories and fortresses, effectively isolating and surrounding the remnants of the Provisional Government. All night reports came in to the third floor of the Smolny Institute:

> A telephone call from Pavlovsk informs me that the government is bringing up from there a detachment of artillery, a battalion of shock troops from Tsarkoye Syelo . . . I order the commissaries to place dependable military defences along the approaches to Petrograd and to send agitators to meet the detachments called out by the government . . . "If you fail to stop them with words, use arms. You will answer for this with your life."

The waiting continued. More key points were taken.

> At the railway terminals, specially appointed commissaries are watching the incoming and outgoing trains, and in particular the movement of troops. No disturbing news comes from there. All the more important points in the city are given over into our hands almost without resistance, without fighting, without casualties. The telephone alone informs us: "We are here!"

The Bolsheviks had indeed arrived. The city was theirs, and only then did Trotsky begin to see the immensity of what had happened . . .

Kerensky fled, and the government disintegrated. His meagre attempts to rally troops failed. The Red Guard had secured the position of the new regime. This Trotsky explained to the Petrograd Soviet at 1 P.M. the following day . . .

Then Lenin appeared before the soviet, coming out of hiding for the first time since the July days. He received a "tumultuous welcome," according to Trotsky, and restored some semblance of belief in the future . . .

Lenin's initial pronouncements established his government's programme. It restated the same objectives he had proclaimed shortly after his return to the Finland Station in April: peace, bread and land. The peasants were seizing the land anyway. Bread required peace, and that was the first order of business. The Bolsheviks immediately approached the German Army with a request to negotiate a cessation of hostilities. A ceasefire was agreed on 3 December 1917.

Peace at Brest-Litovsk

Germany demanded domination of most of European Russia; this Trotsky refused to accept, and after a month he walked out of the talks.

"No peace, no war" was his slogan. The Germans knew better, and simply moved their Army further into Russia, forcing the Bolsheviks to accept even harsher terms in March 1918. By then the last and decisive phase of the war was about to begin.

"African Americans Join the Military"
By James Clyde Sellman
From Encarta Africana

The role of African American soldiers in World War I is about discrimination, but it is also about determination, as historian James Clyde Sellman argues in this selection. Despite the fact that more than 350,000 black Americans were willing to fight for their country, they still had to overcome the prejudice of fellow white soldiers. Few African Americans were in actual combat; most served as support troops. Although African American soldiers were deeply appreciated by the French, many white Americans struggled with fighting alongside black people. When the war was over, 171 African Americans were awarded the French Legion of Honor, but not one single black soldier was given the United States' Congressional Medal of Honor. It would take decades to rectify that oversight.

One of the biggest contributions African Americans made to the war was the introduction of jazz and blues music. Most regiments had bands with African American members, and a number of troops truly enjoyed hearing their music during the quieter moments of the war. The most famous band of all traveled with the 369th Infantry and was led by James Reese Europe, a musician who brought not only music to the soldiers but also an exciting new style of dancing.

In 1919, Emmett J. Scott wrote Scott's Official History of the American Negro in the World War. *After being a private secretary to Booker T. Washington for eighteen years, he served as special assistant to Secretary of War*

Newton Baker during the war. Scott's 500-page book gives a thorough history of the contributions African Americans made to the ongoing battle.

———□———

For most African Americans, the United States' entry into World War I in the Spring of 1917 held the promise that patriotic service could improve their opportunities and treatment in postwar America. W. E. B. Du Bois, the nation's principal African American leader, called on fellow blacks to "close our ranks shoulder to shoulder with our white fellow citizens." Unstinting patriotism, he wrote, would result in "the right to vote and the right to work and the right to live without insult."

Before they could fight the Germans in Europe, however, blacks had to face the opposition of many white Americans. Sen. James K. Vardaman (D-Mississippi) condemned any mobilization plan that would result in "arrogant, strutting representatives of black soldiery in every community." Black leaders had to overcome considerable resistance, especially from southern Democrats, to their insistence that African Americans be included in any wartime draft. Ultimately, their efforts were successful, and 367,710 African Americans were drafted during the war. By this time, however, blacks in the American military had come to expect little in the way of recognition for their service in any branch of the armed forces. Few African Americans served in the U.S. Navy and none in the Marine Corps. The army was strictly segregated, maintaining four black units, the 24th and 25th Infantry and the Ninth and Tenth Cavalry Regiments—all under the command of white officers.

When posted in the western and southern United States, African American soldiers faced harsh treatment, intimidation, and lynching—yet no white citizen was ever punished for engaging in such assaults. On the other hand, in the 1906 Brownsville Affair, 167 black enlisted men were discharged without honor after a Texas shooting incident in which the men quite likely had no part. President Theodore Roosevelt ordered the discharges despite the regiment's recent and courageous service in Cuba and the Philippines during the Spanish-American War of 1898.

As the nation mobilized for war, African American leaders faced great difficulties in furthering the opportunities for blacks within the armed services. In light of the service academies' longstanding hostility to black cadets, the National Association for the Advancement of Colored People (NAACP) pressed for the establishment of a training school for black officers. NAACP efforts resulted in the establishment of a Colored Officers' Training Camp (COTC) at Fort Dodge in Des Moines, Iowa. During the war, Fort Dodge trained and commissioned 639 African American officers. Although symbolically important, the existence of these black officers did little to alter the great racial imbalance: African Americans comprised 13 percent of active-duty military manpower during the war, but only seven-tenths of 1 percent of the officers.

Black aspirations were dealt a further setback when members of the Third Battalion of the 24th Infantry took part in the Houston Mutiny of August 23, 1917—the first race riot in American history in which more whites than blacks died. The violence left 16 whites and four black soldiers dead. After hasty courts-martial, 19 more African American soldiers were executed for their part in the mutiny, and numerous others received lengthy jail sentences. Lt. Col. (Ret.) Michael Lee Lanning, author of *The African-American Soldier*, concluded that a key factor in the riot was, ironically, the previous transfer of 25 of the battalion's most senior sergeants to Des Moines to attend COTC, leaving only one experienced company first sergeant and seriously undermining battalion discipline. In the years to come, this incident effectively undermined any proposal to increase the role of black troops.

African Americans did find greater opportunities once the nation entered the war, which had been ongoing in Europe since August 1914. Many southern blacks moved to the North to take industrial jobs created by the wartime economy. Their numbers added to what would later be known as the Great Migration, a population movement that created or greatly augmented black communities in many northern cities. In addition, 200,000 black soldiers were deployed to Europe, some serving with the American Expeditionary Force and others detailed to the French Army. But the vast majority of these troops were relegated to Services of Supplies (SOS) units and labor battalions. The War Department did not order its four black regiments to Europe, evidently in response to the Brownsville Affair and the Houston Mutiny. Rather than taking part in World War I, the army's most experienced soldiers remained at their posts along the Mexican border.

Instead the army organized two new black combat divisions, the 92nd and 93rd Divisions, through which some 40,000 soldiers saw combat in Europe. But Gen. John J. "Black Jack" Pershing, the supreme commander of the

American Expeditionary Force (AEF), evidently had misgivings about using African American combat troops. When the 93rd arrived in France, General Pershing turned the unit over to the French army.

Both the 93rd Division and the French inadvertently benefited from white Americans' unwillingness to serve alongside blacks. The 369th Regiment of the 93rd Division included Lt. James Reese Europe, the black society musician from New York City who organized the regimental band. Lieutenant Europe was the first black officer to lead troops into combat in World War I, and he and his band introduced the French to African American music, preparing the way for a lasting French fascination with jazz.

With the French, the 93rd experienced far greater acceptance and more equal treatment than that provided by the U.S. Army. The unit served heroically throughout the remainder of the war, suffering a casualty rate of 35 percent. The 369th Infantry Regiment spent more than six months on the front lines—longer than any other American unit—during which it neither surrendered an inch of Allied territory nor lost a single soldier through capture. In the 369th alone, 171 officers and men received either Croix de Guerre or Legions of Merit from the French government.

During the war, no black soldier received the Congressional Medal of Honor, America's highest award for military heroism. In 1991, however, President George Bush presented relatives of Cpl. Freddie Stowers with what he termed a "long overdue" Medal of Honor in recognition of Stowers's heroism on September 28, 1918, while serving in

France with the 371st Infantry Regiment, 93rd Infantry Division. Stowers rallied his company after it encountered withering machine-gun and mortar fire that exacted 50 percent casualties and killed or wounded all of the company's more senior officers. After capturing a German machine-gun position in the first trench, Stowers was leading his men against a second trench line when he was mortally wounded by machine-gun fire. Even after being hit, he continued to crawl forward, and when he could crawl no farther, he continued to shout encouragement to his men. Inspired by Stowers's heroism, the company overran the remaining German positions.

Yet despite their record of wartime service, black soldiers faced a hostile and often violent reception on their return from France. The Ku Klux Klan, reborn in 1915, spread for the first time into the North as well as throughout the South. Between 1914 and 1920, a total of 382 African Americans were lynched—in some cases, the victims were newly discharged soldiers still wearing their uniforms. A city official in New Orleans reportedly told a group of returning World War I veterans, "You niggers were wondering how you are going to be treated after the war. Well, I'll tell you, you are going to be treated exactly like you were before the war; this is a white man's country, and we expect to rule it."

There were serious race riots during and after the war, especially in northern cities that had growing black populations—the 1917 riot in East St. Louis, Illinois, for example. In the Red Summer of 1919, riots broke out in more than two dozen cities. Of these, the deadliest by far was the Chicago Riot of 1919, which resulted in the deaths of 23 African Americans and 15 whites, with a total of 520 whites and blacks injured. This wave of violence effectively quashed black hopes for social advance until President Franklin D. Roosevelt's New Deal and, especially, World War II. Yet the war and its aftermath had profound consequences for black culture, setting the stage for the Black Nationalism of Marcus Garvey and the Universal Negro Improvement Association and leading to the emergence of the self-assured and politically militant New Negro, the Chicago jazz and blues scene, and the Harlem Renaissance.

"German-Americans in World War I"
By Nate Williams
1999

As the United States grew closer to entering the war, the atti-tude of some Americans became so staunchly patriotic that they had little to no tolerance for anyone who spoke out against the country or its president. This became abundantly clear with the case of Robert Prager, a German immigrant and coal miner who made the mistake of speaking critically about those very things.

Although the police tried to hide him, an angry mob of more than 300 men and boys tracked Prager down and took him to a hill to hang him. Despite the fact that he swore he was now a loyal U.S. citizen and loyal to his country, they hanged him until he died.

It was a dreadful moment in U.S. history and one that shocked many. While other people who had spoken out against the war had been tarred and feathered, no one had been killed. What makes the event even more disturbing is the fact that all of the men taken to court for this crime were found not guilty, and so their crime went unpunished. It was a painful example of the climate of the country as it wavered on the edge of war.

——□——

Robert Prager moved to the United States from Dresden, Germany, in 1905 and felt a strong sense of loyalty to the United States when war was declared on his homeland in 1917. Working as a miner just outside of Collinsville, Illinois, Prager applied for membership into the local miners union, but was denied because he was suspected to be a German agent who was plotting to blow up the mine in which he worked. After reading a statement pleading Prager's case for membership into the union, a group of local miners forced Prager to show his patriotism by parading through the streets of Collinsville while kissing the American flag and singing the Star Spangled Banner. After being taken into police custody for safety purposes earlier that evening, Prager was found once again by the now drunken and hostile mob and forced back into the streets. The mob marched Prager just outside of town where he was to meet his fate in the early morning of April 5, 1918. The mob threw a rope over a tree branch and tightened the noose around Prager's neck. Over two hundred people watched the murder of this innocent German-American while not trying to stop the culprits.

The police stopped following the mob once they reached the city limits because they had come to the edge of their jurisdiction. Upon learning of the incident, the local chief of police in Collinsville had this to say, "In one way I believe it is a good thing they got Prager. If he had been spirited away by the police I believe the mob would have vented its rage by hanging two or three Collinsville persons who have been suspected of Disloyalty."

This was one of the most radical cases of anti-German sentiment during World War I in the United States, but was unfortunately not the only one. Fearful of German spies from within the national boundaries, the citizens of the United States suspected and persecuted many German-Americans for acts of "disloyalty." From the leaders of the nation down to the most ordinary citizen, they expressed their feelings of distrust toward all German-Americans and their culture. These feelings of distrust resulted in the loss of First Amendment rights for numerous German-Americans, and this discrimination was often sanctioned by the United States government.

Many of the ideas that citizens harbored about German-Americans came directly from the leader of the nation, President Woodrow Wilson. After the outbreak of war in April 1917, Wilson was quoted as saying "if there should be disloyalty, it will be dealt with a firm hand of stern repression." Wilson's implication of German-Americans in the category of "disloyal" is quite evident in many of his speeches. In his State of the Union address on December 7, 1915, he spoke on the issue:

There are citizens of the United States, I blush to admit, born under other flags, but welcomed under our generous naturalization laws to the full freedom and opportunity of America, who have poured the poison of disloyalty into the very arteries of our national life; who have sought to bring the authority and good name of our Government into contempt . . . necessary that we should promptly make use of processes of law by which we may be purged of their corrupt distempers . . . I am urging you to do nothing less than save the honor and self-respect of the nation . . . disloyalty, and anarchy must be crushed out . . . I need not suggest the terms in which they may be dealt with.

One must remember that Wilson made this speech at a time when America was still neutral in World War I. This speech, heard by or read about by many citizens of the nation, could be taken as a mandate to attack German ideas and beliefs. Being the leader of the free world, Wilson had the ability to affect thought processes and attitudes from coast to coast, and the citizens willingly followed their leader in his hunt for disloyalty . . .

Other political leaders also expressed their views on German-Americans. California Congressman Julius Kahn weighed in with his thoughts just twelve days prior to the hanging of Robert Prager, "I hope that we shall have a few prompt hangings and the sooner the better. We have got to make an example of a few of these people, and we have got to do it quickly." Newspaper headlines from the *New York Times* on April 6, 1918, read "Senators favor shooting traitors" and the *Chicago Tribune* on April 18, 1918, read "Cure treason and disloyalty by firing squad." With President Wilson's broad definition of "disloyalty" and the anti-German attitude of many other leaders of the nation, then how were ordinary citizens supposed to react? If attitude really does reflect leadership, then is it really such a mystery that German-Americans were treated with such little respect during World War I? The public was only carrying out the physical acts that were being advocated by the prominent political figures of the United States.

We know that German-Americans were suspected of disloyalty and treasonous acts during World War I, but just how many of these citizens fell into the category of "disloyal" as defined by the Federal Government and the Justice Department? When the United States entered the war in May 1917 there were 4.6 million people living within the national boundaries who were born in countries that were aligned with the Central Powers. By the last day of March 1917, of these 4.6 million people, 11,770 of them were on a list, compiled by the Justice Department, of those who had been suspected of violating neutrality laws. Attorney General Thomas W. Gregory had this to say about the names on the list: "There are a very large number of German citizens in this country who are dangerous and are plotting trouble, men from whom we must necessarily expect trouble promptly of a sinister sort." Comments like these prompted the arrests of sixty-three suspects immediately after war was declared. Under presidential warrant, a total of 6,300 German-Americans were arrested during the period of United States military involvement in World War I, of which most were paroled, but 2,300 of them were interned by military authorities.

The simple, often overlooked fact, that suspected enemy aliens could be denied their right of habeas corpus and arrested by presidential warrant, and not by warrant from a judge or justice of the peace allowed the Justice Department, which is a cabinet level office, to conduct searches and investigations of anyone whom they suspected of being disloyal, even with no real evidence of such activities. One such case involved a German-born conductor of the Boston Symphony Orchestra, Dr. Karl Muck. Considered German by audiences and the Justice Department, Muck began to be harassed by onlookers to his concerts. Having been cleared of any doing wrong or suspicious activity in two Federal investigations, Muck was suddenly arrested on March 25, 1918, and placed in an internment camp and labeled as a "dangerous enemy alien."

As punishment for their disloyal acts, many German-Americans were not placed in internment camps. Instead, and possibly more disheartening for the accused, their citizenship was revoked. Frederick W. Wursterbarth, a naturalized United States citizen of thirty-six years, refused to subscribe to the Red Cross or YMCA fund drives. Wursterbarth claimed that his reason for not taking part in such drives was because he "did not want to injure Germany and did not want the United States to win the war." This statement, coupled with his failure to comply with the fund drives, resulted in cancellation of his certificate of United States citizenship. Another German-born man living near Emporia, Kansas, who defied food regulations by feeding wheat to his livestock and who made "disloyal" remarks had his citizenship taken away because according to the court, "he had not acted in good faith when swearing allegiance to the United States."

Many other retaliatory acts, administered by ordinary citizens, were numerous across the United States. A Florida citizen who had German origins was badly flogged by a citizens' vigilance committee. A tailor of German descent in Oakland, California, was hanged from a tree and let down while still alive by a group known as the Knights of Liberty. A man in San Jose, California, was tarred, feathered, and chained to a cannon for alleged pro-German sentiments. The Knights of Liberty struck once again in Tulsa, Oklahoma, when they tarred and feathered a German-American before giving him fifty lashes and making him promise to leave the city. A German Lutheran pastor was beaten for preaching in German after the city council had forbidden it, and another pastor was publicly flogged for negative comments about local war committees. Flag kissing, public embarrassment, pledges of allegiance, and tarring/feathering incidents were common throughout the nation.

When anything went wrong in any given area, German conspirators were automatically to blame. Dead horses belonging to a Kentucky judge were believed by the owner to have been poisoned and German-Americans were immediately linked to the killings, by the judge himself. Judge George C. Webb saw the accused in this light:

Men of this ilk, who sow the seeds of dissension or work against the United States Government and its people, should be prosecuted, imprisoned, and shot if necessary. There is not a state in the Union that is not infested with German spies, and they do not hesitate at anything to spread German propaganda, which is the most villainous, barbarous, and extensive menace that the country has to cope with.

What makes this situation all the more frightening is that the person who made these comments was in a position to see that the actions that he advocated were carried out against whom he saw fit. Cases of arson were blamed on German-Americans and accusers even went so far as to claim that tiny pieces of glass that were found in bread could be linked back to enemy aliens.

There were also more symbolic ways of linking German-Americans to the military counterparts of the United States across the Atlantic Ocean. For instance, in Ohio, some cities that had street names of German origin changed them to more patriotic names. In Cincinnati, Berlin, Bremen and German streets became Woodrow, Republic, and English streets. Members of the Cleveland YMCA covered the name "German" in the German Hospital's sign with an American flag. They argued that "the word affected [their] appetites." Many German-Americans changed their names to sound more English so that they would not appear to be suspicious. The teaching of the German language was forbidden in many high schools and colleges. All of these incidents and actions lumped together form one of the darkest periods for advocates of universal

Constitutional rights. I am sure that Robert Prager wished in his last moments on earth that civil liberties were universally enforced during this time.

After three weeks of testimony, the twelve man jury of Robert Prager's peers deliberated for an entire forty-five minutes before delivering the verdict in the trial of the eleven defendants who were accused of his murder. They were all acquitted and set free. Despite the judge's best efforts to convince the jury that it was not the loyalty of Robert Prager to the United States that was on trial, the jury ignored the guilt of the eleven men who played a physical part in Prager's hanging. After the verdict was read, a member of the jury had this to say; "Well, I guess nobody can say we aren't loyal now . . . we've done justice of the right sort for Madison County." This case and the subsequent trial are the most riveting instances in which German-Americans were undeservingly dropped to the status of enemy aliens . . .

The Federal Government and other high-profile political leaders paved the way in the persecution of German-Americans and justified their actions with the claim that they were doing what was best for national security. By stomping out the "disloyal," many ordinary citizens were merely doing what they believed the nation's leaders would do if they had the opportunity. An attempt to eradicate an entire culture was made because they were believed to be enemy aliens. There were over two thousand indictments obtained by the Justice Department under the Espionage Act, but not one involved a person who was actually accused of being a spy. This begs the question: who were the real enemies of the freedom that the United States was claiming to be fighting for in World War I? It is quite obvious that German-Americans during this time were treated far more unfairly than necessary by the very people who claimed to be the advocates of freedom.

CHAPTER FOUR

TIME, CONTINUITY, AND CHANGE: PEOPLE IN WAR

"A July Day at St. Julien"
By Alfred Willcox
From Everyman at War
November 17, 2001

Life in the trenches at the western front was worse than most people could imagine. The numbers give some insight into the conditions: 2,533 men died, 9,121 were injured, and 1,164 went missing every single day. By 1915, there were 4 million soldiers living in those conditions—one soldier for every 4 inches (10 centimeters) of ground.

When the men from both sides first created their trenches, they were little more than 6-foot-deep (1.8 metesr-deep), long, muddy holes. As time passed, however, and these trenches went from being hiding places to being homes, they developed into miles-long, amazingly complex systems. The earth taken out to make the trenches was piled in front (parapets) and behind (parados) for defense and supported by multiple sandbags. Dirt floors were covered with wood so men could walk over them without getting muddy.

Each side had rows of trenches with assigned positions for its soldiers. The first trench was called the front line. These held soldiers who were in the most danger of getting injured or killed.

Both sides were using grenades, rifles, machine guns, bayonets, and knives. Later on, they would use tanks and poison gases. The front-line soldiers were rotated in and out of the front trenches as regularly as possible. About 30 feet (9 m) behind them were the cover trenches, which shot artillery shells and helped protect the front line. Another 50 feet (15 m) behind them were rows of support trenches with extra troops and supplies. Running at a 90-degree angle to these were the communication trenches. They were the soldiers' link to first aid, command posts, and food.

Life in the trenches was dirty, cold, and uncomfortable. Soldiers shared space not only with other soldiers but also with rats and lice. The rats stole food and bit the men incessantly. Sanitation was almost nonexistent, and so disease ran rampant, killing men almost as often as weapons of war. Life vacillated between terrifying battles and mind-numbing boredom. When they weren't fighting, soldiers wrote letters home, performed daily duties, cleaned their weapons, slept, sang songs, and told jokes. Unlikely friendships developed and were just as often abruptly ended at the end of the day when someone didn't return.

Between the two sides of trenches existed no-man's-land, a section that varied between 200 and 2,000 feet (61 to 610 m) wide. This area separated the two combatant armies and was the site of countless bloody battles that gained nothing for either side for years. Thousands died during battles that gained less than a half-mile of land. Thousands more would die the next week when that same small piece of land was retaken by whichever side decided to attack across the barren landscape. The waste of humanity cost the European continent a generation of young men.

Letters from these trenches along the Somme survive to bear witness, even as the soldiers who made it home are now long dead. These letters tell of the wretched daily life of the trenches, but also of the common considerations between comrade soldiers. The letter chosen to illustrate here life in the trenches comes from a young British soldier doing his best to stay alive.

Alfred Willcox was a cook with the Royal Sussex Regiment. This outfit saw all its action on the western front. His letter is his account of the day the Thirteenth Sussex (Lowther's Lambs) captured the village of St. Julien during the Third Battle of Ypres.

———□———

We had waited a long time for nine o'clock on that July night of 1917, and now that we were nearing the hour to be off we wanted sleep.

Yet, through the nervous excitement which weeks of preparation had engendered we could doze but fitfully.

On the rat-eaten boards of a dug-out on the canal bank we sprawled, pinned down by our battle clobber. A curtain hung at the door to keep out gas. It also kept out the twilight.

"Can't someone get a blasted light?" Private Smith suddenly exclaimed, and as an answer a match was struck, applied to a piece of four-by-two, which in turn was stuck in the middle of a tin of dubbin. This acted as a candle, and threw a strange eerie light that turned the faces of the twenty of us who were huddled there a pale green, with dark shadows that made holes for eyes.

Smith, who stared vacantly across to my side, broke the silence again.

"God, this makes you think," he said, in a voice which wasn't quite like his own.

"Put a sock in it, Smith," was the solitary answer he received to his philosophy, and once more silence descended upon the dug-out, and shadows jumped over the domed roof as the green light bobbed up and down . . .

There was a tap on the curtain which was lifted as the colonel came in. I don't know where we had picked up the old man, but he was a decent old buck.

"Now, my boys,"—something like that he began—"you've been practising and waiting for this moment for a long time. Try to remember what you have learnt, and keep up the name of the regiment. I've just come to wish you all the best of luck. There'll be some porridge up soon. Fill your bellies. And God bless you."

I hadn't the heart to eat much of the porridge. I stuffed down two or three spoonfuls and dozed off again . . .

I awoke with a start. The light had burnt out. My mate, George, gave me a kick because I wasn't moving.

"Come on," he said; "they're falling in."

"Here, give me a hand. This blasted clobber's weighing me down."

He pulled me up, and with a good deal of clatter we struggled through the little door. There was still a bit of light in the sky, which was reflected in the muddy water of the canal. There was also a suggestion of rain in the wind.

We fell in. The roll was called: we were all there. Then, in single file, we turned left to the communication trench and the enemy's lines.

We reached our positions and waited, sprawling in the Flanders mud on a summer's night. George and I sprawled together to keep warm; for even a summer's night, with the rain in the wind which comes across the plain, Flanders can be chilly . . .

"Stretcher bearers," came a voice.

"Coming up," was the reply.

"Someone hit," muttered George.

"Ay."

"Lucky sod. He's saved a lot of trouble."

I never knew who it was. The poor devil called out for his mother.

"Oh, put a sock in his blasted mouth," came another nerve-racked voice.

The stretcher bearers got the chap away and there was quiet again. Every few minutes the officers came round to see if we were all right. I was more thankful to see the cooks. They had struggled up with hot tea, strengthened with rum.

It was the most liberal treatment we had had during the War. By the way the liquor burned, I should say it was fifty-fifty. The youngest lad in the platoon—he must have lied to get into the Army, poor fool—crawled on his belly and would insist on shaking hands with every one of us. He was thoroughly drunk.

It was still dark, and my illuminated watch said 3.30. That meant half an hour more. Then we became very silent, and even the guns seemed to be still. It seemed like the calm that comes before the thunderstorm . . .

An officer came round once more.

"Five minutes more, boys," he said; "get ready."

We fixed our bayonets. We gripped each other's hands. And waited. My heart seemed to take up that devil's tattoo and thumped against my ribs . . .

Suddenly it came.

I can still hear those three sharp staccato cannon shots which seemed to split the darkness, for there followed a tremendous roar and crash which sent the first light of dawn trembling along the distant horizon above the mist, suddenly to burst into miles of flames.

And from No Man's Land shot up a myriad of distress lights, trembling. And "express trains" roared overhead. It was a wonderful moment. Some magic force drew us up from our crouching positions, and in the blue mist which still clung to the hollows in the battlefield we looked like ghosts wreathed by smoke. Eighty thousand of us.

Then we swept forward as if caught by the wind. The spreading light of dawn caught the glint of bayonets as they moved on and on . . .

I met Ira by the side of a shell hole. He had pulled out his leg from the squelchy mud which had dragged him down to the knee. Months we had campaigned together. The happiness

which we had managed to squeeze out of those dreary
months we shared; the sorrows we shared; the parcels from
home we shared.

On those blessed days of rest we had flung bits of poetry
to each other and had teased to say what we had quoted. We
thought that after the War we would quit the monotonous life
at home and would go adventuring. We had mapped out what
we would do, where we would go—this country and that.

They knew us as the twins. Before we went over we had
been told to press on: if a man dropped down he must be
left—others would follow to patch him up.

"If you fall I shall stop," said Ira to me a day before.
"Hell to them all! I shall stop." But we were separated before
we began. He was attached to another platoon.

I saw him as I went over. He was well.

He laughed as he swore, "What a bloody mess!" We said
good-bye—"God be with you."

I never saw him again.

Later I wrote to him. The letter was returned—
undelivered. The mark of a rubber stamp was on the envelope,
"Killed in action." Just that. A country's regrets to me that my
friend was dead . . .

Most of the firing had been on our side. We did not
know it at the time. There was such a screaming in the air
that lead seemed to be flying everywhere. Something
whipped by and one swore that his ear had been missed by
a hair's breadth.

In front our barrage fell like a curtain and the earth
vomited up mud and dirt. Then the fun began. A rattle, with

that well-known crescendo and diminuendo as the machine gun swept from east to west, cracked out. In front of me I saw a pair of arms go up and a rifle drop and six feet of khaki crumple up.

I saw George hurrying to get behind a scrap of a hedge. He never got there. But he got his "armistik" all right; he got it in the guts. I dropped on my knees and crawled to that little bit of shelter.

I saw stretched at full length, with his face towards heaven, a boy in grey with the down of youth upon his chin.

We were off our track. We turned left and reached a road. It was strange to see abandoned guns and parapets turned the wrong way. Down the road came two other figures in grey. One was leaning heavily upon the other. His shirt was torn off his back and there was a great gash in his flesh. We looked at each other in passing. We spoke to each other only with our eyes and went our ways . . .

There were too many snipers about to be very comfortable, but those of us who kept our heads low survived the hour. Our platoon was like a spearhead in the line. In the early evening the enemy opened out on us; in mistake our own guns opened, too.

"Better fall back a few yards," said the officer, and even as we were doing so something jabbed my hand. It dropped down and blood spurted out.

The others had gone. I was alone. The fire was not continuous. It came in fits and starts. In an interval my good hand helped me out. I dashed out and dropped in the shadow of a grave. I was seen. From the pillbox, hidden somewhere about, which had given us trouble all the day, a couple of bits of lead whistled. I crawled into an enormous shell hole and began to sink into mud.

With the slime clinging to me I got away, through the bottom of a hedge which, by the grace of God, had remained there. No one to be seen now and my head facing I knew not where.

A great, livid waste, the light of day going, and the way might be to the north or the south. I had lost my bearings.

Not far away a tank, half embedded, was getting it full tilt.

The sweat stood on my dirty face. And then in that great expanse of mud and wire I spotted a little red cross on a little flag, sticking eighteen inches out of the ground.

I felt safe again.

It was at the entrance to a cellar. The cellar was filled to overflowing. Men and bits of men were huddled there or stretched at full length.

"Better get on," said the doctor, noticing that my legs were whole. So, duly labelled, I turned to home again. I passed my mates with waterproofs on their shoulders, standing to.

I tried to run, but felt weak. Suddenly a barrage fell in front of me. I turned into the remains of a cottage by the side of the road, found a seat on an empty petrol tin in the corner, pulled down my tin hat to cover my face. But, like some venomous beast, the barrage crept nearer and soon bits of the brick wall began to fall. I was shaking with fright.

I decided to bolt the moment the barrage lifted. My arm was throbbing with pain. My leg had gone to sleep. I thumped it with my other hand—and life came back again and with it hope. There came a flash. I shut my eyes. A deafening crash and tumble of mortar. The firing stopped.

I bolted. Down the road zigzag, zigzag, to dodge the snipers, on and on nearer home. Soon I saw the white tapes. I followed. My throat was burning with thirst. I saw a watercart in a ditch and soon water was running down a long throat that asked for more and more.

In the early hours of the morning I tumbled into an electrically lighted dug-out dressing station two miles from the front line where there were clean bandages and steaming tea. I fell at full length, motionless. Someone pressed drink to my lips.

The journey was not ended. Soon they came to carry me on again.

"Got a couple of Jerries here. Do you mind if they go with you?"

Mind? Not if it was the whole German Army. They bundled us in together and we were off. The rain was falling piteously. At the field ambulance we were taken out. The place was full. Hope and despair lived there side by side.

There were screams as the broken bodies were lifted on to the tables for the surgeons' knives. There was a great light on dirty faces of men as they sat on wooden forms, their arms bared to the doctor who pricked the flesh with his inoculating needle to carry its serum to attack the tetanus germ.

They took us to a tent on which the rain beat down ceaselessly and mercilessly. I fell on a stretcher and pulled the damp blanket on top of me. What did it matter? Rain-rain-rain. Far away the guns growled. Rain-rain-rain.

It splashed on to the canvas and dripped into the tent.
Drip-drip-drip. Each drip seemed to fashion itself into a
word—sleep. Sleep-sleep-sleep. Nearly twenty-four hours after
the attack. To-morrow the hospital train—and Blighty. But
now sleep. Sleep. Sleep. Sleep. S-l-e-e-p.

Oh, thank God! Thank God, s-l-e-e-p.

"On 'Loving Thine Enemy'"
Author unknown
From The Literary Digest
March 13, 1915

*It was such a supremely unusual moment in the history of
war that it has achieved mythical status. Yes, the Christmas
Truce truly did happen, and even today, almost a century
later, it remains a powerful story.*

*The first Christmas since the war began was coming
closer. The Senate had suggested a twenty-day truce over the
holiday, but the idea was dismissed as impossible. The same
attitude met Pope Benedict XV's suggestion of a cease-fire
over Christmas Day. Everyone assumed that the war would
continue on December 25 just as it would the day before and
the day after.*

*However, everyone was wrong. As Christmas Eve
opened across the trenches at the western front, a change
came over the land. German soldiers made the first move,
lighting candles on trees. Before long, the British, French,
Belgians, and Germans were all singing Christmas carols,
and the sound drifted across no-man's-land to the opposite*

side. What irony, they all must have thought at the time, to be singing of peace and goodwill toward man while amid the nightmare landscape of a scarred battlefield.

Even more remarkable, the soldiers mutually laid their guns down—without orders, committees, or commanders telling them to—and crossed the war-torn no-man's-land to talk to each other, share food and drink, even exchange gifts. A few spontaneous games of soccer popped up, and there was an air of friendship and peace, as those carols suggested.

When the troops were ordered to return to fighting, most refused. Those that did pick up their weapons simply shot them harmlessly overhead.

This remarkable night of the Christmas Truce was one that captured the hearts of people all over the world, yet it would never be repeated. By the following winter, both sides knew that this battle was not ending anytime soon, and the camaraderie disappeared. Nonetheless, it was a moment that would not be easily forgotten.

——□——

The Christmas Truce was a bad thing for the soldiers, from a military standpoint. It showed them the ironic futility of standing up to kill men with whom they could just as readily hobnob over exchanged cigars and chocolate. Berlin wrote an order to stop such proceedings, and we have the opinion of an English major that "if you wanted to end this war, all you'd have to do would be to let the men have another truce or two like that Christmas one. They'd get to talking to each other, and suddenly they'd decide that the whole business was foolishness and they'd lay down their guns and go home." Nothing shows better than this the fact asserted by William G. Shepherd in the *New York Evening Sun* that the soldiers who stand face to face in opposing trenches do not hate one another. The *London Times* published a number of letters from the trenches setting forth the state of affairs that existed on Christmas day. One of them from an officer in a Highland regiment to his family at home may be taken as typical:

"You need not have pitied us on Christmas day; I have seldom spent a more entertaining one, despite the curious conditions. We were in the trenches, and the Germans began to make merry on Christmas even, shouting at us to come out and meet them. They sang songs (very well); our men answered by singing, 'Who Were You with Last Night?' and of course 'Tipperary' (very badly). I was horrified at discovering some of our men actually had gone out, imbued more with the idea of seeing the German trenches than anything else; they met half-way, and there ensued the giving of cigarets and receiving of cigars, and they arranged (the private soldiers of one army and the private soldiers of the other) a forty-eight hours' armistice. It was all most irregular, but the Peninsular and other wars will furnish many such examples; eventually both sides were induced to return to their respective trenches, but the enemy sang all night, and during my watch they played 'Home, Sweet Home,' and 'God Save the King,' at 2.20 AM! It was rather wonderful; the night was clear, cold, and frosty, and across to our lines at this usually miserable hour of night came the sound of such tunes very well played, especially by a man with a cornet, who is probably well known.

"Christmas day was very misty, and out came those Germans to wish us 'A Happy Day'; we went out, told them we were at war with them, and that really they must play the game and pretend to fight; they went back, but again attempted to come toward us, so we fired over their heads, they fired a shot back to show they understood, and the rest of the day passed quietly in this part of the line, but in others a deal of fraternizing went on. So there you are; all this talk of hate, all this fury at one another that has raged since the beginning of the war, quelled and stayed by the magic of Christmas. Indeed, one German said: 'But you are of the same religion as we, and to-day is the Day of Peace!' It is really a great triumph for the Church. It is a great hope for future peace when two great nations, hating each other as foes have seldom hated, one side vowing eternal hate and vengeance and setting their venom to music, should on Christmas day, and for all that the word implies, lay down their arms, exchange smokes, and wish each other happiness! Beyond all this, the day itself was rendered impossible for war by mist. So altogether I expect we had a better time than all you poor things at home, who were probably bothering your heads thinking of the chances of war and the discomfort of trenches. Next year, pray God, we shall all be round the fire and at peace."

Next day, we read, the men had to be shifted to new positions, or there would have been no fighting. It is quite clear from this that the gospel of hate can gain adherents only among those who remain at home to meditate instead of going forth to fight. A singular instance is afforded by a Lutheran pastor, Dr. Julius Schiller, of Nuremberg, who describes himself as a Royal Protestant pastor. In the *Vossische Zeitung* (Berlin) he observes that before the war it was considered immoral to hate; but now "Germans know that they not only may, but they must, hate." Herr Lissauer's "Chant of Hate" against England is, he declares, a faithful expression of the feelings cherished in the depth of the German soul. Further:

"All protests against this hate fall on deaf ears; we strike down all hands that would avert it. We can not do otherwise; we must hate the brood of liars. Our hate was provoked, and the Germans can hate more thoroughly than any one else. A feeling that this is the case is penetrating into England, but the fear of the German hate is as yet hidden. There is a grain of truth in Lord Curzon's statement that the phlegmatic temperament of his countrymen is incapable of hating as the Germans hate. We Germans do, as a matter of fact, hate differently than the sons of Albion. We Germans hate honorably, for our hatred is based on right and justice. England, on the other hand, hates mendaciously, being impelled by envy, ill-will, and jealousy. It was high time that we tore the mask from England's face, that we finally saw England as she really is."

The pastor further declares that the day of judgment for this world is at hand, and the honorable task or carrying the judgment into effect has been entrusted to Germany. He claims that Germany hates "with a clean conscience." And—

"[W]e, who are fighting for truth and right with clean hands and a clean conscience, must have him on our side who is stronger than the strongest battalions. Hence our courage and our confidence in a fortunate outcome of the

world-conflagration. The dawn will soon appear that
announces that the 'Day of Harvest' for Germany has broken."

A Telegram from the American Consulate General in Petrograd to the U.S. Secretary of State
March 20, 1917

By 1917, Russia was in rather dire straits. Conditions in the country were dismal. Inflation was climbing unchecked and, when combined with growing food shortages, causing the people to revolt. Every day, women lined up for nearly eight hours to get their bread rations. When even bread began to run out, trouble was inevitable. One day, in Petrograd (now St. Petersburg), the Russian capital at the time, women began to riot, gathering supporters as they went.

In growing numbers, protesters took to the streets, and the anger spread like an uncontrollable wildfire. For the next several days, thousands of people voiced their anger and frustration at what was happening in their country. When Czar Nicholas saw this, he talked to General Khabalov, the chief of the military. He ordered his soldiers to shoot into the crowds to control the people. Many of the soldiers refused to follow that command. Those who did, however, turned a riot into an escalation of violence between the people and the Russian government. Discontent that had occupied the country's people for years was overspilling from homes, factories, and offices into the streets. The nation neared collapse under the shear weight of oppression pushed to an unbalanced posture like that of a bowling pin. A revolution had arisen from within over the most basic needs of society: food. This whole incident proved to the czar that changes were coming and he was powerless to stop them. Eventually, he abdicated and handed control of the country to Prince Lvov. This action set the course for the Bolshevik Revolution and eventually for the complete reversal of positions when Russia switched from the side of the Allies to that of the Central powers.

Such little information came out of Russia during these tumultous times that the facts of the Bread Riots, such as we know these, came from a consular letter sent from the American embassy in Petrograd to the secretary of state in Washington, D.C. As consular letters go, this particular description is in depth to an extent that the story of these desperate Russians comes through as a historical response of a people who are tired of being oppressed by their government.

———□———

Petrograd, Russia, March 20, 1917
(Confidential)
SUBJECT: Revolutionary Movement in Petrograd.
THE HONORABLE
The Secretary Of State
WASHINGTON
SIR:

I have the honor to report that as a result of serious economic, political, and military disturbances, the government of this city and district has been completely assumed by an Executive Committee of the Imperial Duma at least for the time being.

On the beginning of the week of March 4th, a shortage of black bread was noticeable. This at once caused unrest among the laboring classes. All other prime necessities within the means of the working classes had already gradually disappeared as the winter advanced: meat, sugar, white flour, buckwheat, potatoes. Fish, fowls, eggs, milk, cheese, and butter had for a long time been so expensive that they were only within the means of the very well-to-do classes. The unrest first took visible form in the outskirts and factory districts of the city Wednesday, March 7th, when the workmen struck after the dinner hour and met in groups to discuss the situation.

The next day, Thursday March 8th, there were spontaneous isolated demonstrations. In many places, a few of the working class, mostly women, tired of waiting in the bread lines in the severe cold began to cry, "Give us bread." These groups were immediately dispersed by large detachments of mounted police and cossacks.

March 9th, large crowds of women marched to the Kazan Cathedral (opposite the Consulate) with bared heads, still crying for bread and shouting to the police "Give us bread and we will go to work." This crowd was peaceable and was dispersed.

Saturday morning the crowds, composed of working men and students visibly with a serious purpose, came from all districts to the center of the city. Besides calling for bread, these crowds shouted "Down with the Government," "Down with the Romanoffs," and occasionally "Down with the War." The mounted police endeavored to drive the mobs from the Nevsky, the main street, but resistence was made and barracades built on the side streets. The police withdrew after firing on and charging the crowds with whips without success. Their place was taken by infantry who fraternized with the people. Announcement was made by the police that after 6 o'clock that day, all groups of persons would be fired upon. The crowds did not disperse, and street battles took place, especially on the Nevsky, resulting in great loss of life.

At this time the infantry and cossacks refused to fire on the crowds or to charge them. Towards evening a detachment of cossacks actually charged and dispersed a body of mounted police.

Sunday, when it became known that the Emperor had proroged [postponed] the Duma and that it had refused to recognize this order, there was disorganized and sporadic fighting all over the city, with heavy loss of life. The unmounted police were withdrawn from the streets. Many regiments which had been locked in their barracks, mutinied, during the night, killed some of their officers, and marched to defend the Duma, which was still sitting. By Monday the disorganized riots developed into a systematic revolutionary movement on the part of the working men and the constantly growing numbers of mutinied troops, to capture the city of Petrograd. The fighting moved rapidly across the city from the Duma as a center, so that by Monday night, only isolated houses and public buildings, upon which machine guns were mounted, were held by the police and the few remaining loyal troops. At midnight the Duma had announced that it had taken the government into its own hands and had formed an Executive Committee to be the head of the temporary government.

Tuesday and Wednesday the fighting was confined to volleys from machine guns fired by the police from the isolated house tops, public buildings and churches, and the return fire by the soldiers, such fighting continuing until all police were taken. Violence necessary in arresting government, army and police officials, took place at this time.

During these two days the fighting around the Consulate was severe, and on several occasions it seemed as if nothing could save the Singer Building from total demolition. Machine guns were presumably being operated from points of advantage in this building by police agents, as well as from neighboring buildings, the revolutionists replying with volleys from their rifles and machine guns mounted in automobiles.

At 4:30 o'clock Monday afternoon troops, always without officers, entered the building. All the business offices in it had been deserted early in the day, except the Consulate. When the soldiers reached the third floor they were shown the location of the Consulate by one of the staff. They insisted on seeing the balconies of the Consulate, and several soldiers, with members of the Consulate staff entered the Consulate and satisfied themselves that no machine guns were located there. No damage was done in the Consulate, but other offices and the building itself were considerably injured.

Notice was given that kerosene would be poured on the building and burned. At 5:30 o'clock the Consulate was closed after everything of importance had been placed in the safe and notices posted on all the doors, stating that the nature of the office was foreign and contained only property of the United States Government. The staff left the building under heavy fire and with a guard.

At 6:30 o'clock, when the firing had ceased, it was arranged to have a Consulate employee constantly on duty, day and night. This alone saved the Consulate from being violated, for Tuesday and Wednesday there was no order in the city and the Singer building was visited five times by armed soldiers, many of whom were intoxicated, looking for weapons.

A military guard has now been furnished the Consulate and the office is intact, and safe for the present at least. The fact that the Consulate is not in a separate building owned by the American Government is particularly unfortunate in this city, there the question of protection of Americana is so apt to arise and where prejudices against firms located in the same building endangers the Consulate and the lives of the staff.

The Singer building has been under suspicion since the beginning of the war as being German, the masses believing the Singer Company to be a German corporation.

I have had to defend the American eagle on the top of the building, as it was believed to be a German eagle and the crowd intended to tear it down until I explained in Russian the difference between the American and German eagle.

The Consulate is keeping in touch with the members of the American colony, none of whom up to the present have been injured. As the Consulate is not at all suitable for housing purposes, having no kitchen, bath or sleeping accomodations, I have notified the members of the Colony that in case they are turned out of their homes or hotels or have to leave for protection, they may come to my home, which is centrally located, where I could protect them and make them fairly comfortable.

I shall make only a limited report of observations on the political situation leading up to the economic situation in this district. It being supposed the Embassy has already cabled a report in the matter.

Immediately following the assumption of national authority by the Executive Committee of the Duma, the Council of Workmans' Deputies challenged its exclusive authority. This council is a body which existed secretly during the old regime and represented the revolutionary workmen. Spontaneously a third authority appeared in the Council of Soldiers' Deputies which soon merged with the workmens' council under the name of the Council of Workmen's Soldiers' Deputies.

Tuesday, Wednesday, and Thursday, (the 13th, 14th, and 15th,) were, up to the present, the most critical times of the revolution, when there was immediate danger of civil war in Petrograd between the Duma and the Council of Workmens' and Soldiers' Deputies. This crisis passed however, when, late on Thursday afternoon, a provisional agreement was reached. This agreement was based on a temporary ministry chosen from the members of the Duma with a political program of eight points:

1. Immediate political amnesty.

2. Immediate freedom of press, speech, meeting, the right to strike;—these rights to be extended to soldiers insofar as compatible with military organization.

3. Immediate abolition of all caste, religious, and race difficulties.

4. Immediate preparation for a constitutional convention to determine the permanent form of national government.

5. Immediate substitution of militia with elective officers, under control of local self-governing bodies in place of the old police system.

6. Election to local self-governing bodies by universal direct, equal, and secret suffrage.

7. Retention of arms by revolutionary soldiery, the soldiery not to be removed from Petrograd.

8. Retention of strict military discipline during actual service with full civil freedom to soldiers when not on duty.

On the 15th of March the Emperor abdicated for himself in favor of his brother the Grand Duke Michael. On the 16th the Grand Duke Michael declined the throne unless it should be offered him by the Constitutional Convention. This again averted further civil war as it put all parties in agreement to await the Constitutional Convention.

The old police which was maintained by the national government as a part of the Ministry of the Interior, has been replaced by the City Militia, a volunteer organization under the auspice of the National Duma and the Board of Aldermen. It is now maintaining order throughout the city and cooperating with the Commissariats in the various wards. The Commissariats are under the control of the Council of Workmen's and Soldiers' Deputies, which still sits in conjunction with the National Duma.

Passport regulations for foreigners have not been changed and are controlled by a new Gradonatchalnik (Chief of City or Chief of Police) who is now, as formerly, dependent on the Ministry of the Interior.

A new Mayor has been chosen by the Aldermen. He is attempting to control and improve the local food supply which is again the danger point as at the beginning of the revolution. All necessities have to be brought to Petrograd from the provinces and a serious food shortage now exists. If it is not relieved at once it will cause further serious disorders capable of developing into new revolutionary movements with greater socialistic tendencies than heretofore.

Today, March 20th, for the first time in ten days, a very few electric street cars are running but not enough to constitute a resumption of the service. The workmen have not returned to the factories as was hoped.

I have the etc. ["the honor to be, Sir, Your obedient servant," is crossed out]

North Winship [signature]

["American Consul." is crossed out]

"Nurse Edith Cavell"
By Peter Clowes
From Military History Magazine
August 1996

Although the women of this era did not raise weapons and engage in face-to-face combat, their lives were nonetheless dramatically changed by the war. Millions of women lost their husbands, their sons, and their fathers. In addition to this, they had to face all new demands on their time and talents. Before the war, more than three-quarters of women worked within their homes, but this was no longer possible. With

*most able-bodied men off to war, it was up to the women to
replace them at work. Women were now the breadwinners for
their families and found themselves doing everything from
driving buses to standing in factory lines. A great many of
the women in the United States were put to work in munitions factories producing parts of weapons that would eventually reach the battlegrounds.*

*In Britain, thousands of women did go to the front,
although not to fight alongside husbands, brothers,
boyfriends, and fathers. Accepted in the army, navy, and air
force, they went as nurses, cooks, and ambulance drivers.
French women headed to factories and fields, as well as to
hospitals to help with the war effort for any chance to shorten
the war—or at least make it easier to fight for those soldiers
caught in the cauldron of battle. In Germany, women were
not allowed to go to the front, but they served their country
by setting up nurseries so other women could work and produce ammunition. They even built an underground train system. Edith Cavell was an English nurse, and today she is
considered one of England's heroines. During her time as
matron of a Red Cross hospital in Brussels, she helped Allied
soldiers reach neutral Holland. The Germans caught her, and
her punishment was death by firing squad. Her last words
were, "Standing, as I do, in the view of God and eternity, I
know now that patriotism is not enough. I must have no
hatred or bitterness towards anyone."*

———□———

One gray, dismally wet night in November 1914, two British
soldiers in disguise were guided through the silent side

streets of German-occupied Brussels by a patriotic Belgian civilian. Herman Capiau was an engineer by trade, but since the outbreak of World War I he had played a key role in an escape organization that was sheltering British and French soldiers trapped behind the German lines after the Allied defeat at Mons.

One of the soldiers, Lt. Col. Dudley Boger, who had a leg wound, had grown a beard in the three months he had been lying low, and was wearing the black hat and floppy tie of a typical Belgian factory worker. His colleague, Company Sgt. Maj. Frank Meachin, also dressed as a laborer, had packed rolls of cloth between his shoulders to turn himself into a hunchback. That, he hoped, would explain to any inquisitive German soldier why such a tall, strongly built man was not serving in the army.

Capiau cautiously led the pair across the greasy cobbles. German patrols were frequent, and he was forced to try three different routes before reaching the Berkendael Medical Institute, a training school for nurses on the outskirts of the Belgian capital.

The three men were admitted into the building, and Capiau handed a letter of introduction to the school's matron, a British nurse named Edith Cavell. There was a brief, hushed conversation, then Capiau left the matron's office and slipped away into the night. It was 8 PM. Sister White, the assistant matron, was summoned.

"These men are fugitive soldiers," Cavell told Sister White. "Give them beds in the empty surgical house." Both men, Sister White later recalled, looked dirty and tired, and she put them to bed immediately.

Boger and Meachin were the first of more than 200 British, French and Belgian troops who would be hidden and cared for by Cavell and her staff during the next 12 months.

When they were taken prisoner, Boger and Meachin, both of the 1st Battalion, Cheshire Regiment, had been taken to a temporary hospital in a convent at Wiheries, Belgium. But when their guards' backs were turned, the two men had staggered out into the village under cover of darkness and hid in a disused building.

The fugitive soldiers were in a difficult position. Many other officers and men of the British Expeditionary Force had been cut off from their units and left behind in the retreat from Mons. Some, aided by civilians, had reached the Belgian coast. But when Antwerp fell, the Belgian army had retired to link up with British units on their right, and had opened sluice gates behind them to flood the low-lying country and hold up the German army's advance. That also had cut off the escape route to the coast for stranded Allied soldiers.

Peasants, priests and nuns cared for some of the fugitive troops. Unwounded Allied soldiers who disguised themselves as laborers or miners risked being shot as spies—a danger Boger and Meachin were prepared to face.

They had been lucky to contact a helpful Roman Catholic priest who led them to the home of a woman named Libiez, the widowed mother of a local lawyer, and she had hidden them in the loft of an outbuilding at the bottom of her garden for several weeks.

All occupied countries have their share of traitors. On October 26, 1914, German intelligence received a tip that

Libiez was concealing two British soldiers. Within hours, a company of cycle troops of the Landsturm swooped into town and searched both Libiez's home and those of her neighbors. Twice they returned, but the fugitives had been alerted in time and had slipped out to mingle with a crowd of curious Belgian civilians in the street.

Boger and Meachin were clearly embarrassing their gallant host, and the following night two nuns, Sister Marie and Sister Madeleine, arrived with a hurricane lamp to guide them to a convent in Wasmes.

Libiez's son—a member of the Belgian escape organization—then took over escort duties and accompanied the British soldiers into Mons, where they stayed three days at the home of Louis Dervaire in the Rue de la Gare. There, they had their photographs taken and were given fake civilian identity cards. Capiau then escorted them to Cavell's institute on November 1.

Edith Cavell was one of the most fascinating characters of World War I. Forty-seven years old when Boger and Meachin met her, she had been born in a large Georgian-style farmhouse in the English village of Swardeston in the county of Norfolk. Her father, a vicar, was a strict Victorian.

Cavell first worked as a governess for a family in Brussels, then became a nurse. By 1911, she was training nurses for three hospitals, 24 schools and 13 kindergartens in Belgium. She was a brisk, businesslike, rather straight-laced woman with a high crown of graying hair and gray eyes.

Her sense of duty bordered on the fanatical, and she demanded the highest standards from her pupil nurses. She kept a watch before her at breakfast; any girl more than two minutes late would be ordered to work an extra two hours. She was often "cold, distant and aloof," according to one of her staff.

In August 1914, Cavell was spending a short holiday with her mother, who was then living in Norwich after her husband's death. Edith was weeding her mother's back garden when she heard the dramatic news that Germany had invaded Belgium. "I am needed more than ever," she said, and immediately left for the Continent. Her mother never saw her again.

Cavell and her staff were hard at work at the training school in the suburbs of Brussels when the German army occupied the city. All 60 British nurses were ordered home, but Edith somehow remained behind. German nurses arrived to replace the British nurses and, together with all the remaining Belgian girls, were sent out to hospitals in the city as required.

It was contrary to Cavell's nature to refuse help to anyone in distress, and Boger and Meachin were hidden in the institute for two weeks. When Cavell heard that the Germans were going to search the building, she ordered Sister White to take the soldiers to an empty house in nearby Avenue Louise. Sister White then came under German suspicion and wisely decided to leave the country. Just before Christmas 1914, she crossed the Dutch frontier—carrying military information for the British, obtained by Colonel Boger, hidden in her underclothes.

Cavell still considered Boger and Meachin to be in danger and, with the help of two English civilians living in Brussels (who so far had been left alone by the German authorities), arranged for them to be accompanied by a guide out of the city. Boger, still lame, was to travel down the canals to the border aboard a coal barge, while the sergeant major, who could walk but could not speak French, would be disguised as a peasant collecting fish in Holland.

The two soldiers stayed together as far as Ghent. Meachin made friends with a Belgian smuggling newspapers across the frontier into neutral Holland, reached the border and made a dash for it. Eventually, he got back to England, returned to the front and was awarded the Distinguished Conduct Medal.

Colonel Boger was recaptured when German soldiers raided a cafe where he was having a drink; he was sent to a POW camp at Ruhleben for the rest of the war. He was later awarded the Distinguished Service Order.

At the Berkendael Institute, more fugitive soldiers arrived and all received help from Cavell. But the danger that the Germans would discover the secret of the institute grew daily. British soldiers staying there were warned not to go out. Nevertheless, one night several of them walked to a cafe down the road and got drunk. Before long, it became widely known that Cavell was harboring British and French troops under her roof.

Despite an order from the German authorities that anyone sheltering Allied troops would be shot, Cavell's secret work continued. She wrote to her cousin, "I am helping in ways I may not describe to you till we are free."

It became obvious, however, that the escape route could not be kept open indefinitely. The Germans were well aware that large numbers of fugitive soldiers were crossing the Belgian border into Holland. Then, in August 1915, the

Germans raided the home of Philippe Baucq, a member of the escape organization, and arrested him. Unfortunately, Baucq failed to destroy several incriminating letters in which Edith Cavell's name appeared.

The head of the escape organization, Prince de Croy, left his large country chateau near Mons to warn colleagues in Brussels. He called on Cavell in her office and told her he was going into hiding. "I expect to be arrested," she said firmly. "Escape for me is futile and unthinkable." The prince realized it was hopeless to try to dissuade her and departed, eventually managing to cross the border to safety.

On August 5, Otto Mayer of the German secret police arrived in the Rue de la Culture. Cavell was driven to police headquarters and questioned. But nothing of importance was found in the institute—Cavell had, in fact, sewn her diary inside a cushion.

There is some controversy over the confession Cavell made to Mayer. On being told that other members of the organization—35 had been arrested—had admitted their guilt, she spoke freely about the help she had given to Allied soldiers. "Had I not helped," she said later in a letter from her prison cell, "they would have been shot." Cavell was accused of conducting soldiers to the enemy and was tried by a military court in Brussels. Although more than 200 troops had passed through her hands, the only document incriminating the nurse was a tattered postcard sent, rather unwisely, by an English soldier thanking her for helping him to reach home. Cavell was sentenced to death, along with four Belgians.

Two firing squads, each of eight men, carried out the execution at dawn on October 12, 1915, at the national rifle range in Brussels. Cavell was still wearing her nurse's uniform.

The words she spoke to her last English visitor, Stirling Gahan, the English chaplain in Brussels, became almost as famous as Admiral Horatio Nelson's at Trafalgar. "I know now that patriotism is not enough," she said. "I must have no hatred and no bitterness towards anyone."

Although the German action was justified according to the rules of war, the shooting of Edith Cavell was a serious blunder. Within days, the heroic nurse became a worldwide martyr, and the Germans were universally described as "murdering monsters." As a result of her execution, Allied morale was strengthened, and recruitment doubled for eight weeks after her death was announced . . .

CHAPTER FIVE

GLOBAL CONNECTIONS: ON THE BATTLEFIELD, IN THE TRENCHES

"Memoirs & Diaries: The First Gas Attack"
By Anthony R. Hossack
From Everyman at War
1930

Perhaps one of the most brutal and compelling images people have of the First World War is the use of poison gases. In a war that already included the most sophisticated weaponry and equipment the world had ever imagined, this was the most frightening. It was silent, almost invisible, and deadly. Even though gases killed only about 30,000—far fewer than those killed with traditional weapons—it was still the weapon that most terrified soldiers and civilians alike.

The first time a poison gas was used was in April 1915. It was a chlorine-based gas that had been developed by Fritz Haber, considered Germany's top chemist. The Germans released 168 tons from 6,000 cylinders at Ypres in Belgium. Heavier than air, it crept along the ground in a yellowish green cloud, seeping into trenches, reaching more than 4 miles (6.4 km) and attacking 10,000 French, British, and Canadian men. Its effects were quick and merciless.

Later, the Germans manufactured different kinds of poison gas, trying to find the most effective one. They released one with phosgene, which smelled pleasantly like newly mown hay but was nevertheless lethal. The Allies produced gas masks to counteract the effects, and then it became a race. As soon as an effective mask was developed, the Germans created a different kind of gas. Cloth masks soaked in thiosulphate neutralized the effects of chlorine, so the Germans released another gas, which caused severe vomiting. As soon as a soldier inhaled it, he ripped off his mask to vomit and was overcome by the other gases.

Mustard gas was one of the cruelest inventions. It created first- and second-degree burns on whatever it contacted—including the lining of eyes and throats. In addition, it was long lasting, soaking into the soldier's clothes and presenting continued danger for several weeks. Gas masks continued to improve. Goggles were added to protect the eyes, nose clips prevented inhaling through the nose, and filters with charcoal and soda lime helped protect the lungs. The masks were uncomfortable, but they were relatively effective and certainly better than the alternative.

The Allies attempted making their own poison gases and even released one at Loos, Belgium, in September 1915. However, they quickly learned one of the biggest disadvantages to using a gas for a weapon; it is uncontrollable. When the wind shifted, they lost many of their own men.

This selection is a firsthand account of surviving a gas attack. Anthony R. Hossack served first with the Queen Victoria Rifles from 1915 along parts of the western front. In the last year of the war, he was taken prisoner in the battle for Mt. Kemmel while attached to the M.G. Battalion of the Ninth (Scottish) Division.

———□———

It was Thursday evening, April 22nd, 1915. In a meadow off the Poperinghe-Ypres road, the men of the Queen Victoria Rifles were taking their ease. We had just fought our first big action in the fight for Hill 60 . . .

Now some of us were stretched out asleep on the grass, others making preparations for a much-needed toilet. Our cooks were preparing a meal, and on our right a squad of Sappers were busily erecting huts in which we were to sleep. Alas! We never used them! As the sun was beginning to sink, this peaceful atmosphere was shattered by the noise of heavy shell-fire coming from the north-west, which increased every minute in volume, while a mile away on our right a 42-cm [17 in] shell burst in the heart of the stricken city of Ypres.

As we gazed in the direction of the bombardment, where our line joined the French, six miles away [9.7 km], we could see in the failing light the flash of shrapnel with here and there the light of a rocket. But more curious than anything was a low cloud of yellow-grey smoke or vapour, and, underlying everything, a dull confused murmuring.

Suddenly down the road from the Yser Canal came a galloping team of horses, the riders goading on their mounts in a frenzied way; then another and another, till the road became a seething mass with a pall of dust over all.

Plainly something terrible was happening. What was it? Officers, and Staff officers too, stood gazing at the scene, awestruck and dumbfounded; for in the northerly breeze there came a pungent nauseating smell that tickled the throat and made our eyes smart. The horses and men were still pouring down the road, two or three men on a horse, I saw, while over the fields streamed mobs of infantry, the dusky warriors of French Africa; away went their rifles, equipment, even their tunics that they might run the faster.

One man came stumbling through our lines. An officer of ours held him up with levelled revolver, "What's the matter, you bloody lot of cowards?" says he. The Zouave was frothing at the mouth, his eyes started from their sockets, and he fell writhing at the officer's feet. "Fall in!" Ah! we expected that cry; and soon we moved across the fields in the direction of the line for about a mile [1.6 km]. The battalion is formed into line, and we dig ourselves in . . .

About midnight we withdrew from our temporary trenches and marched about for the rest of the night, till at dawn, we were permitted to snatch what sleep we could under a hedge.

About the middle of the morning we were on the move again, to the north, and were soon swinging along through Vlamertinghe. About two miles [3.2 km] out of that town we halted in a field. By this time we had joined up with the remainder of our Brigade, the 13th, and, after a meal had been served, we were ordered to dump our packs and fall in by companies. Here our company commander, Captain Flemming, addressed us.

"We are," he said, "tired and weary men who would like to rest; however, there are men more weary than we who need our help. We may not have to do much; we may have to do a great deal. Whatever happens, fight like hell. I shall at any rate." A few moments more—then off we go again towards that incessant bombardment, which seemed to come closer every minute.

The Scottish Borderers led the Brigade, followed by the Royal West Rents, then ourselves—all with bayonets fixed, for we were told to be prepared to meet the Germans any- where on the road.

We were now in the area of the ill-fated French Colonial Corps. Ambulances were everywhere, and the vil- lage of Brielen, through which we passed, was choked with wounded and gassed men. We were very mystified about this gas, and had no protection whatever against it.

Shortly after passing through Brielen we turned to the left down a road which led to the Canal, along the south side of which ran a steep spoil bank, and, as the head of our battal- ion reached this, we halted. We could see nothing of what went on on the other side . . .

All night there seemed to be a spasmodic bombardment all round the Salient. Next morning about 12 o'clock the Adjutant, Captain Culme-Seymour, was chatting to Captain Flemming a few paces away from where I was lying, when up rushed a breathless despatch rider and handed him a message, which he read aloud to Flemming.

I caught three words, "Things are critical." In about five minutes the Colonel had the battalion on the move. We moved off in double file by companies, our company leading; as we did so a big shell burst in the midst of "D" Company, making a fearful mess.

We moved on quickly, like a gigantic serpent, with short halts now and then. As we skirted Ypres there was a roar of swift-moving thunder and a 17-inch [43 cm] shell, which seemed to be falling on top of us, burst a quarter of a mile away, covering us with dirt.

Over meadows and fields green with young crops which would never be harvested, past cows peacefully grazing that had had their last milking, we went, passing curiously unperturbed peasants, who watched us from the farms and cottages.

As we crossed the Roulers road a lone cavalryman came galloping down it, hatless and rolling in his saddle as though drunk. Some wag throws a ribald jest at him. He turns his ashy face towards us, and his saddle it seems is a mass of blood. Above us a Taube appears and, hovering over us, lets fall a cascade of glittering silver like petals. A few moments more and shells begin to fall about us in quantities, and gaps begin to appear in our snakelike line.

We pass a field battery; it is not firing, as it has nothing to fire, and its commander sits weeping on the trail of one of his useless guns. We quicken our pace, but the shelling gets heavier. It seems to be raining shrapnel. Captain Flemming falls, but struggles to his feet and waves us on with encouraging words.

We double across a field, and in a few moments come on to the road again. Here was action indeed, for barely had we reached the road and started to work our way towards St. Julien, than we found ourselves amongst a crowd of Canadians of all regiments jumbled up anyhow, and apparently fighting a desperate rearguard action.

They nearly all appeared to be wounded and were firing as hard as they could. A machine gun played down the road. Then comes an order: "Dig in on the roadside." We all scrambled into the ditch, which, like all Flanders ditches, was full of black, liquid mud, and started to work with entrenching tools—a hopeless job.

A woman was bringing jugs of water from a cottage a few yards away; evidently she had just completed her week's washing, for a line of garments fluttered in the garden.

"Dig! Dig, for your lives!" shouts an officer. But, dig! How can we? 'Tis balers we need.

A detonation like thunder, and I inhale the filthy fumes of a 5.9 [centimeter charge] as I cringe against the muddy bank. The German heavies have got the road taped to an inch. Their last shell has pitched on our two M.G. teams, sheltering in the ditch on the other side of the road. They disappear, and all we can hear are groans so terrible they will haunt me for ever.

Kennison, their officer, stares dazed, looking at a mass of blood and earth. Another crash and the woman and her cottage and water jars vanish and her pitiful washing hangs in a mocking way from her sagging clothes line. A bunch of telephone wires falls about us. To my bemused brain this is a catastrophe in itself, and I curse a Canadian Sapper beside me for not attempting to mend them.

He eyes me vacantly, for he is dead. More and more of these huge shells, two of them right in our midst. Shrieks of agony and groans all round me. I am splashed with blood.

Surely I am hit, for my head feels as though a battering-ram has struck it. But no, I appear not to be, though all about me are bits of men and ghastly mixtures of khaki and blood. The road becomes a perfect shambles. For perhaps half a minute a panic ensues, and we start to retire down the road. But not for long. Colonel Shipley stands in the centre of the road, blood streaming down his face. The gallant Flemming lies at his feet, and the Adjutant, Culme-Seymour, stands in a gateway calmly lighting a cigarette.

"Steady, my lads!" says the Colonel. "Steady, the Vics! Remember the regiment." The panic is ended.

"This way," says Seymour. "Follow me through this gate here." As we dash through the gate, I catch a glimpse of our M.O. working in an empty gun-pit like a butcher in his shop. Many were the lives he saved that day.

Once through the gate we charge madly across a field of young corn. Shrapnel and machine-gun bullets are cracking and hissing everywhere. Ahead of us is a large farm, and advancing upon it at almost right angles to ourselves is a dense mass of German infantry.

We are carrying four extra bandoliers of ammunition as well as the rest of our equipment. Shall I ever get there? My limbs ache with fatigue and my legs are like lead. But the inspiring figure of Seymour urges us on, yet even he cannot prevent the thinning of our line or the gaps being torn in it by the German field gunners, whom we can now plainly see.

At last we reach the farm, and we follow Culme-Seymour round to its further side. The roar of enemy machine guns rises to a crazy shrieking, but we are past caring about them, and with a sob of relief we fall into the farm's encircling trench.

Not too soon either, for that grey mass is only a few hundred yards off, and "Rapid fire! Let 'em have it, boys!" and don't we just. At last a target, and one that we cannot miss. The Germans fall in scores, and their batteries limber up and away. At last we have our revenge for the discomfort of the afternoon. But the enemy re-form and come on again, and we allow them to come a bit nearer, which they do. We fire till our rifles are almost too hot to hold, and the few survivors of our mad quarter of an hour stagger back.

The attack has failed, and we have held them, and thank God that we have, for, as our next order tells us, "This line must be held at all costs. Our next is the English Channel."

And hold it we did, through several more big attacks, though the enemy set fire to the farm and nearly roasted us, though our numbers dwindled and we were foodless and sleepless, till, thirty-six hours later, we were relieved in a misty dawn, and crept back through burning Ypres for a few hours' respite.

"Belleau Wood: One Man's Initiation"
From In Many a Strife: General Gerald C. Thomas and the U.S. Marine Corps, 1917–1956
By Allan R. Millett
1993

When United States Marine Corps major general George Barnett persuaded the War Department to allow a group of marines to go to France in 1917, he had no idea what was about to ensue. Although there were a tragic number of losses at this infamous battle, it was also one of the marines' finest moments.

The unit that went to Belleau Wood came to be known as the Fourth Brigade of the Second Division. It included a headquarters, a machine-gun battalion, and two infantry regiments. Under the command of James Guthrie Harbord, they were instructed to capture Belleau Wood, which had been controlled by the Germans at the western front for quite some time. It was not an easy assignment. The marines had to cross a pasture and open wheat field, and there was little to no protection there. On June 6, 1918, they headed out, and they lost more marines that day than any other single day in history (until 1943). Only twenty of the marines that went in emerged unhurt. Between the marines and the army, 1,600 were taken as prisoners of war, and 9,500 men died. The marines took, lost, and then retook the area at least a half a dozen times, including the nearby villages of Vaux and Bouresche, finally defeating the Germans. They did such an admirable job that Belleau Wood was renamed Bois (Wood) de la Brigade de Marine. It became known as one of the marines' most historic battles.

This selection follows the experience of one man, Gerald C. Thomas, a marine at the scene of Belleau Wood. He would end up serving in the marines until 1955 and would play a part in three different wars.

———□———

For the 1st Battalion, 6th Marines, the battle began around six o'clock in the morning on June 10 and did not end until it left the wood seven days later, an exhausted, smaller, but still combative group of veteran Marines. Jerry Thomas fought with his battalion from start to finish. He learned to cope with stress, fear, hunger, thirst, exhaustion, and the death of friends over a protracted period of combat. The fighting on June 10 struck hard at Thomas's 75th Company, which moved through the wood with Lieutenant Overton's 76th Company on the left, in the center of the battalion front. When the company struck a strongpoint of three German machine guns, Thomas lost a dozen comrades from the 3d Platoon. The Marines crawled forward through "a great mass of rocks and boulders," Thomas later recalled, until they could throw grenades at the machine-gun nests.

Through most of the day, Thomas remained with Hughes at the battalion PC to manage scouting missions and analyze the vague company reports. During the afternoon the regimental intelligence officer, First Lieutenant William A. Eddy, came forward and told Hughes that Colonel Lee wanted an accurate report of the German positions. Taking Thomas with him to prepare sketch maps, Eddy crawled around the woods and quickly learned that no one could see much through the brush. Then, against Thomas's advice, he climbed a tree. Eddy immediately tumbled from the branches into Thomas's lap and said, "My God! I was looking square at a German in a machine-gun nest right down in front of us!" Eddy and Thomas returned to Hughes to report that the Germans still held Hill 181, a rocky rise that divided the western and southern wheat fields. Any attack across the western wheat field would still meet flanking fire from

Belleau Wood. Having taken thirty-one casualties in the wood on June 10, Hughes agreed with Eddy's assessment that one battalion could not clear out the remaining Germans.

General Harbord then committed the 2d Battalion, 5th Marines, to the battle, establishing its attack for four-thirty the next day. Hughes's left-flank company, Overton's 76th, was supposed to protect the right flank of Wise's battalion. Hughes assigned Thomas the job of ensuring that Overton contacted Wise's battalion as Harbord directed and "conformed to the progress of the attack," as noted in the brigade attack order. As the rolling barrage lifted, Thomas and one of his scouts left the wood and found Wise's battalion moving across the same deadly wheat field that had become the graveyard of Berry's battalion on June 6. Its passage was only slightly less disastrous. As the battalion neared Belleau Wood, German artillery fire crashed down upon it and machine-gun fire raked its front and flanks. Instead of pivoting to the north, the Marines plunged straight ahead into the wood's narrow neck and across the front of the 1st Battalion, 6th Marines, which had joined the attack, too.

Pressured by his own company commanders for help, Wise asked Thomas where the 76th Company was and why it had not appeared on his right flank. Off Thomas went again, back into the wood. He found Overton, whose company was indeed in action and successfully so. Under Overton's inspired and intelligent direction, the 76th Company had destroyed the last German positions around Hill 181 and opened Belleau Wood for Wise's battalion. Overton found

Wise's anger mildly amusing and wondered why the 5th Marines could not use the available cover. Certain that Overton had the situation under control, Thomas returned to Hughes's PC and told Johnny the Hard that the 76th Company had fulfilled its mission.

The two-battalion battle for Belleau Wood became a muddled slugfest, with Wise moving east when he should have been moving north. His battalion engaged the strongest German positions, and suffered accordingly. At one point, Wise, Lee, and Harbord all thought that the Marines had seized Belleau Wood. Hughes knew better, but his battalion had its own problems as the Germans responded to the attack with intense artillery fire and reinforcing infantry . . .

In the early morning of June 13, the Germans mounted heavy counterattacks on the Marines, punishing positions on the 1st Battalion's left flank, still held by the 76th Company. Macon Overton asked battalion headquarters to investigate the fire to the rear, since he thought it might be coming from the disoriented 2d Battalion, 5th Marines. Etheridge and Thomas, who were reconnoitering the lines, decided to check Overton's report. Working their way through the wood, which was now splintered and reeking of cordite smoke and souring corpses, they found an isolated 5th Marines company

The commander, a young lieutenant named L.Q.C.L. Lyle, told him that he was sure the firing came from bypassed Germans. He had no contact with the company to his left. Etheridge volunteered to scout the gap in the 5th Marines' lines, but before he and Thomas had moved very far, they saw some Germans who had just killed a group of Wise's Marines and occupied their foxholes. Before the Germans could react with accurate rifle fire, the two Marines sprinted back to Lyle's position and told him about the Germans. Lyle gave Etheridge a scratch squad armed with grenades, and Thomas and Etheridge led the group back through the wood until they again found the German position. In the short but intense fight that followed, the Marines killed four Germans and captured a sergeant, who showed them another German stay-behind position, which the 6th Marines attacked and wiped out later the same day. Impressed with Thomas's performance in this action, Hughes had him cited in brigade orders for bravery in combat.

The German prisoner also provided Thomas with a temporary reprieve from battle, for brigade headquarters wanted to interrogate the POW immediately. Hughes ordered Thomas to escort the sergeant to the rear. When he arrived at the brigade PC, Thomas reported to Harbord's aide, Lieutenant R. Norris Williams (in civilian life, a nationally known tennis player). Williams asked him when he had last eaten a real meal. Thomas knew exactly: five days. The lieutenant sent him to the brigade mess, where a sergeant who had obviously not been missing his meals fixed Thomas a large plate of bacon, bread, and molasses, accompanied by hot coffee. Food had seldom tasted so good . . .

The effects of sleep deprivation, hunger, and thirst were severe, exacerbated now by gas attacks. The Marines fought in their masks, but had to remove them often to clear condensed water and mucus, increasing the chances of inhaling gas. They simply endured burns over the rest of their bodies. The Germans tried no more infantry counterattacks, but they pummeled the battalion with heavy mortars and Austrian 77mm [3 in] cannon, which fired a flat-trajectory, high-velocity shell dubbed a "whiz bang." In the meantime, Wise's battalion (or rather its remnants) and the 2d Battalion, 6th Marines, had finally reached the northern section of Belleau Wood, but could advance no farther without help. The 1st Battalion, 6th Marines, completed the occupation and defense of the southern woods. On June 15 the battalion learned it would finally be replaced, by a battalion of the U.S. 7th Infantry. Two days later, at less than half their original strength, they shuffled out of Belleau Wood . . .

For the 1st Battalion, 6th Marines, the battle for Belleau Wood really ended when the battalion returned to the rest area at Nanteuil-sur-Marne on June 17, but it did not leave the sector until the entire division departed in early July On the road to Nanteull, the battalion found its kitchens and enjoyed hot stew ("slum") and café au lait that tasted like a five-star meal. For three days the battalion did little but sleep and eat. The Maine River became a welcome Marine bathtub. Ten-day beards and dirt came off; thin faces and sunken eyes took longer to return to normal.

The battalion returned to the Belleau Wood sector on June 20–21 in order to give Harbord two fresh battalions in brigade reserve. The battle in the northern wood had grown as the Germans committed a fresh regiment, and Harbord had countered with an attack by the 7th Infantry and the 5th Marines. After the 5th Marines' attacks finally cleared the north woods on June 26—Harbord could report accurately "Belleau Wood now U.S. Marine Corps entirely"—the battalion marched back into the wood, a doleful walk through the clumps of unburied German and American dead. Except for occasional harassing shell fire, the battalion did not have to deal with live Germans, although the smell of the dead ones was bad enough.

Jerry Thomas spent most of his time in the PC or checking the battalion observation posts. His last special duty in Belleau Wood was to help guide the U.S. 104th Infantry, 26th Division, into the sector. Learning that the relieving "Yankee Division" had already lost men to German artillery fire, he once again proved his intelligence and force by persuading an army lieutenant colonel to move the 104th Infantry into the wood by a longer but more protected route than the one the colonel intended to use. Thomas had no desire to add more Americans to the 800 or so dead who were scattered throughout the 6th Marines' sector.

Just as dawn was breaking, the 1st Battalion left Belleau Wood for the last time. "Led by our chunky commander, Major Garrett, we traversed the three quarters of a mile to Lucy at a ragged double time." Pushing along on his weary legs, Sergeant Jerry Thomas turned his back on Belleau Wood, at last certain that he would never see it again, at least in wartime. The battle, however, had made him a charter member of a Marine Corps elite, the veterans of the Battle of Belleau Wood. From this group the Marine Corps would eventually draw many of its leaders for the next forty years, including four commandants (Wendell C. Neville, Thomas

Holcomb, Clifton B. Cates, and Lemuel C. Shepherd, Jr.). On June 10, 1918, Jerry Thomas had entered Belleau Wood a sergeant whose early performance in France had marked him as a courageous and conscientious noncommissioned officer. He left the wood a proven leader of Marines in combat, a young man clearly capable of assuming greater responsibilities in the most desperate of battles.

Speech to the U.S. Senate
By Henry Cabot Lodge
August 12, 1919

Despite America's undisputed victory in the war, there were plenty of people who still disagreed with President Wilson's political decisions. Perhaps one of the most vocal and recognized opponents was Henry Cabot Lodge. Lodge was a Republican senator from Massachusetts and the Senate majority leader. President Wilson proposed the possibility of sponsoring the new League of Nations, an intergovernmental organization that had been set up at the Paris Peace Convention in 1919. Although its goal was an ideal one—to promote international peace and security—Lodge did not feel that the United States should be part of it. After its participation in the war, he believed the country needed to stay away from international political issues, and the people tended to agree with him. The country was beginning to lean toward a philosophy of isolationism, a national policy that focused on staying out of political affairs outside of the United States.

Lodge felt so strongly about not being part of it that he campaigned against the League of Nations as often—and as vocally—as he could. In the speech below, made to the Senate on August 12, 1919, he argued against America's involvement with it. At the same time, Wilson was campaigning for the opposite point of view. He went on a transcontinental tour of almost 10,000 miles (16,093 km) to convince the people that participating in the League of Nations was a good decision for the country. In the middle of his journey, he collapsed; a week later, he had a severe stroke that left him partially paralyzed. His power and influence were fading, and his position on the League of Nations faded right along with him. In the end, the United States did not join the League of Nations, which was established in 1920. A mere twenty-five years later, the United Nations was formed to replace it.

———▫———

Mr. President:

The independence of the United States is not only more precious to ourselves but to the world than any single possession. Look at the United States today. We have made mistakes in the past. We have had shortcomings. We shall make mistakes in the future and fall short of our own best hopes. But none the less is there any country today on the face of the earth which can compare with this in ordered liberty, in peace, and in the largest freedom?

I feel that I can say this without being accused of undue boastfulness, for it is the simple fact, and in making this treaty and taking on these obligations all that we do is in a spirit of unselfishness and in a desire for the good of mankind. But it is well to remember that we are dealing with nations every one of which has a direct individual interest to serve, and there is grave danger in an unshared idealism.

Contrast the United States with any country on the face of the earth today and ask yourself whether the situation of the United States is not the best to be found. I will go as far as anyone in world service, but the first step to world service is the maintenance of the United States.

I have always loved one flag and I cannot share that devotion [with] a mongrel banner created for a League.

You may call me selfish if you will, conservative or reactionary, or use any other harsh adjective you see fit to apply, but an American I was born, an American I have remained all my life. I can never be anything else but an American, and I must think of the United States first, and when I think of the United States first in an arrangement like this I am thinking of what is best for the world, for if the United States fails, the best hopes of mankind fail with it.

I have never had but one allegiance—I cannot divide it now. I have loved but one flag and I cannot share that devotion and give affection to the mongrel banner invented for a League. Internationalism, illustrated by the Bolshevik and by the men to whom all countries are alike provided they can make money out of them, is to me repulsive.

National I must remain, and in that way I like all other Americans can render the amplest service to the world. The United States is the world's best hope, but if you fetter her in the interests and quarrels of other nations, if you tangle her in the intrigues of Europe, you will destroy her power for good and endanger her very existence. Leave her to march freely through the centuries to come as in the years that have gone.

Strong, generous, and confident, she has nobly served mankind. Beware how you trifle with your marvellous inheritance, this great land of ordered liberty, for if we stumble and fall freedom and civilization everywhere will go down in ruin.

We are told that we shall "break the heart of the world" if we do not take this league just as it stands. I fear that the hearts of the vast majority of mankind would beat on strongly and steadily and without any quickening if the league were to perish altogether. If it should be effectively and beneficently changed the people who would lie awake in sorrow for a single night could be easily gathered in one not very large room but those who would draw a long breath of relief would reach to millions.

We hear much of visions and I trust we shall continue to have visions and dream dreams of a fairer future for the race. But visions are one thing and visionaries are another, and the mechanical appliances of the rhetorician designed to give a picture of a present which does not exist and of a future which no man can predict are as unreal and short-lived as the steam or canvas clouds, the angels suspended on wires and the artificial lights of the stage.

They pass with the moment of effect and are shabby and tawdry in the daylight. Let us at least be real. Washington's entire honesty of mind and his fearless look into the face of all facts are qualities which can never go out of fashion and which we should all do well to imitate.

Ideals have been thrust upon us as an argument for the league until the healthy mind which rejects cant revolts from them. Are ideals confined to this deformed experiment upon a noble purpose, tainted, as it is, with bargains and tied to a peace treaty which might have been disposed of long ago to the great benefit of the world if it had not been compelled to carry this rider on its back? "Post equitem sedet atra cura [black care sits behind the rich man on horseback]," Horace tells us, but no blacker care ever sat behind any rider than we shall find in this covenant of doubtful and disputed interpretation as it now perches upon the treaty of peace.

No doubt many excellent and patriotic people see a coming fulfilment of noble ideals in the words "league for peace." We all respect and share these aspirations and desires, but some of us see no hope, but rather defeat, for them in this murky covenant. For we, too, have our ideals, even if we differ from those who have tried to establish a monopoly of idealism.

Our first ideal is our country, and we see her in the future, as in the past, giving service to all her people and to the world. Our ideal of the future is that she should continue to render that service of her own free will. She has great problems of her own to solve, very grim and perilous problems, and a right solution, if we can attain to it, would largely benefit mankind.

We would have our country strong to resist a peril from the West, as she has flung back the German menace from the East. We would not have our politics distracted and embittered by the dissensions of other lands. We would not have our country's vigour exhausted or her moral force abated, by everlasting meddling and muddling in every quarrel, great and small, which afflicts the world.

Our ideal is to make her ever stronger and better and finer, because in that way alone, as we believe, can she be of the greatest service to the world's peace and to the welfare of mankind.

"The Roots of World War II"
By Sheldon Richman
February 1995

A number of historians believe that World War I was little more than a prelude to World War II. They feel the time in between was simply an elongated truce. Although the Allies and Central powers agreed to and signed the Treaty of Versailles, it was done out of necessity, not out of a true desire to end the battle. Several nations put their signatures on the paperwork but walked away vowing revenge anyway. The country hardest hit by President Wilson's 440-article-long treaty was Germany. By signing it, Germany was agreeing to things that would invariably plunge the country into chaos. The treaty demanded complete disarmament, an end to its overseas colonies, and a cessation of munitions and weapons production. The two most difficult parts of the

treaty, however, were the financial reparation and the damn-
ing "war guilt clause."

The Treaty of Versailles demanded that Germany admit
in writing that it had been the one to start the war. It was
humiliating for the country to take on the complete blame,
and it was an embarrassment that would tarnish the pride of
Germany's people and image to the rest of the world. When
the treaty was signed, the overall cost of the war had not
been figured yet. Eventually, that amount was computed, and
it came to an astounding $33 billion. The treaty decreed that
it was Germany's responsibility to pay back that money—an
impossible task. However, if Germany failed, a harsh system
of punitive measures would be initiated.

Germany walked away from World War I with burdens
it was not prepared to handle and with enemies who were just
biding their time until the next opportunity to strike. That
chance came two decades later when the powder keg that
became known as World War II exploded.

Historian Sheldon Richman puts these facts, grievances,
and premonitions into the perspective of a counterfactual
argument. What if some events had not taken place or if
those events had turned out differently? The hinges of histroy
often turn on a single response to a large problem. So
Richman asks, "What if Wilson had kept the United States
out of the war?"

———□———

It is commonly thought that the 20th century witnessed two
world wars. It would be more accurate to say that the century
had but one world war—with a 21-year intermission. To put it

another way, World War II grew out of World War I; indeed, it was made virtually inevitable by it. More specifically, a case can be made that World War II was a result of American intervention in the First World War.

Counterfactual history is a risky endeavor. But the events that followed America's entry into World War I strongly suggest that had President Woodrow Wilson permanently "kept us out of war," as his 1916 presidential campaign slogan boasted, the conditions that produced World War II would not have been sown.

The Great War began in August 1914. America did not enter the war until April 1917. By that time both sides were exhausted from years of grinding warfare. There is ample reason to believe that had nothing new been added to the equation, the belligerents would have agreed to a negotiated settlement. No victors, no vindictiveness.

But it was not to be.

The messianic President Wilson could not pass up what he saw as a once-in-a-lifetime opportunity to help remake the world. As historian Arthur Ekirch writes in *The Decline of American Liberalism*, "The notion of a crusade came naturally to Wilson, the son of a Presbyterian minister, imbued with a stern Calvinist sense of determinism and devotion to duty." He was goaded by a host of Progressive intellectuals, such as John Dewey and Herbert Croley, editor of *The New Republic*, who wrote that "the American nation needs the tonic of a serious moral adventure."

On the other side, the opponents of war understood what, ironically, Wilson himself pointed out in private just before asking Congress for a declaration of war: "War required illiberalism at home to reinforce the men at the front. We couldn't fight Germany and maintain the ideals of Government that all thinking men shared."

Wilson was right. Within months, the United States had conscription, an official propaganda office, suppression of dissent, and central planning of the economy (a precedent for Franklin Roosevelt's New Deal).

While Wilson said the United States was going to war to make the world safe for democracy, he in fact entered for the less lofty principle of making it safe for American citizens to sail on the armed ships of belligerents. Regardless, what matters here is the effect U.S. intervention had on the war.

Aside from the general exhaustion of the warring nations, a major development was occurring to the east. The war had caused great hardship in Russia. Food was in short supply. Workers went on strike, and housewives marched in protest. Army regiments mutinied. In March 1917, Czar Nicholas II abdicated, and when his brother refused the throne, a provisional, social democratic government was set up in Russia. As historian E. H. Carr wrote, "The revolutionary parties played no direct part in the making of the revolution."

Despite the people's revulsion, Alexander Kerensky's provisional government stayed in the war at the insistence of the Allies and Wilson, who by then had sent American boys to Europe. When Lenin returned to Russia from Zurich, he made his Bolsheviks the one antiwar party in the country. This gave Lenin the opportunity to become the world's first communist dictator. An earlier negotiated settlement would have eased the Russians' misery and probably averted the second revolution. Lenin immediately accepted Germany's peace terms, including territorial concessions, and left the war. (Toward the end of the war, the Allies invaded the new Soviet Union, ostensibly to safeguard war materiel. The invasion created long-lasting distrust of the West.)

Thus, the first likely consequence of U.S. prolongation of the war was the Bolshevik Revolution (and the Cold War). Communism—its threat of worldwide revolution and its whole-sale slaughter—was a key factor in the rise of the European despotism that sparked World War II. (Had the Bolsheviks come to power anyway and Germany had won the war, Germany would have thrown the communists out.)

Entry of fresh American power gave the advantage to the Allies, and Germany signed the armistice in November 1918. Before allowing that, Wilson, in the name of spreading democracy, demanded that the Kaiser go. The president thus was responsible for the removal of what would have likely been an important institutional obstacle to Hitler and his aggressive ambitions.

The armistice set the stage for the Paris Peace Conference and the Treaty of Versailles. Article 231 of that Treaty—the infamous war guilt clause—said:

> The Allied and Associated Governments affirm and Germany accepts the responsibility of Germany and her allies for causing all the loss and damage to which the Allied and Associated Governments and their nationals

have been subjected as a consequence of the war imposed upon them by the aggression of Germany and her allies.

Germany was to become an outcast nation on the basis of its war guilt. The problem was that Germany was not uniquely guilty. World War I was the product of a complex political dynamic in which nations other than Germany—Russia and France, for example—played important roles. Nevertheless, Germany was branded as the perpetrator.

The victors imposed crushing reparations on Germany for the cost of the war. That was contrary to Wilson's original, nonpunitive program (The Fourteen Points) and to the prearmistice agreement with Germany. But at the peace conference, he acquiesced to England and France in order to achieve his dream of a League of Nations. Adding to the humiliation was the Allied occupation of the Rhineland and the tearing away of German-speaking areas in order to reconstitute Poland and create Czechoslovakia. Moreover, the treaty nullified German control in the East, which Lenin had conceded, removing what would have been a formidable barrier against Bolshevism.

Not all the hardship resulted from the treaty. During the war the Allies imposed a starvation blockade on Germany. Due to French insistence, that blockade remained in place until the treaty was signed in June 1919. The German people were made to watch their children starve for six months after the guns fell silent. The blockade killed an estimated 800,000 people.

In the 1920s, many people—Germans and others—would call for revision of the unjust treaty. But no one in a position to do anything about it heeded the call. Can one imagine ground more fertile for the growth of the poisonous vine called Nazism?

The second likely consequence, then, of U.S. prolongation of the war was the rise of Nazi Germany.

Other consequences can be speculated on. For example, Murray Rothbard has argued that the Federal Reserve System engaged in a prolonged postwar inflation of the money supply in order to help Great Britain restore its prewar gold-Pound relationship. That inflation led to the crash of 1929 and the Great Depression. Perhaps if the United States had refrained from entering the war, and if a negotiated settlement had been reached, the Fed would not have felt obliged to assist Britain in achieving its unrealistic aims.

We can now do an accounting of the likely consequences of U.S. intervention in Europe: communism in Russia (and everywhere else it later reverberated), Nazism in Germany, the Great Depression, the New Deal, and World War II (not to mention the Cold War and the growth of the American leviathan).

No one would suggest that Woodrow Wilson foresaw those consequences and intervened anyway. But the intelligent men who warned that war would lead to revolution and totalitarianism were vindicated. The war critic Randolph Bourne observed that "it is only 'liberal' naivete that is shocked at arbitrary coercion and suppression. Willing war means willing all the evils that are organically bound up with it."

And what if U.S. forbearance had not permitted a negotiated settlement and Germany had won the war? Aside from the fact that Wilson's closest adviser, Col. E. M. House, saw no threat to the United States from a German victory, we can best answer that question with another question: Who would not trade the events of 20th-century military and political history for the Kaiser?

TIMELINE

1914 — Archduke Franz Ferdinand is assassinated in Sarajevo on June 28.

Austria-Hungary declares war on Russia on July 28.

Britain declares war on Germany and Austria-Hungary on August 4.

The First Battle of the Marne is fought September 5–10.

The First Battle of Ypres is fought in October and November.

Unofficial Christmas Truce is called on the western front on December 25.

1915 — Germany declares a submarine blockade of England on February 4.

The Second Battle of Ypres is fought from April 22 to May 5. Chemical weapons are used for the first time.

Lusitania is sunk on May 7.

1916 — Battle of the Somme takes place from July 1 to November 18.

Woodrow Wilson is reelected on November 7.

1917 — President Wilson gives his "Peace without victory" speech on January 22.

Unrestricted submarine warfare is declared by Germany, again, on February 1.

1917 —— Czar Nicholas II abdicates on March 15.

Russia collapses March–September.

The United States declares war on Germany and enters the First World War on April 6.

Aquaba is captured by Arabs led by T. E. Lawrence on July 6.

The German-Russian armistice is reached on December 3.

1918 —— President Wilson delivers his Fourteen Points speech to Congress on January 8.

Treaty of Brest-Litovsk is signed by Soviet Russia and the Central powers (Germany, Austria-Hungary, and Turkey) on March 3.

Bolsheviks murder Czar Nicholas II and his family on July 16 and 17.

Allies break through the Hindenberg line on September 29.

Kaiser Wilhelm abdicates on November 9.

The Allies accept the Fourteen Points on November 5.

World War I ends on November 11. The Central powers are forced to annul the Brest-Litovsk Treaty.

FOR MORE INFORMATION

The Great War Society
P.O. Box 18585
Stanford, CA 94309
Web site: http://www.worldwar1.com
An organization dedicated to studying World War I and its
influences on the twenty-first century.

Over There!
c/o Bill Hoffman
16601-D Gothard St.
Huntington Beach, CA 92647
A publication devoted to information about World War I.

The Western Front Association
96 College Ave.
Poughkeepsie, NY 12603
Web site: http://www.wfa-usa.org
An organization dedicated to the war's western front and its
implication in today's culture and politics.

Woodrow Wilson Birthplace Foundation
18-24 N. Coalter St./P.O. Box 24
Staunton, VA 24402
Web site: http://www.woodrowwilson.org
Detailed information about the president who led the United
States in most of the war.

FOR FURTHER READING

Clare, John D, ed. *First World War* (Living History). San Diego: Gulliver Books, 1995.

Hatt, Christine. *World War I (1914–1918)*. New York: Franklin Watts, 2001.

Hipperson, Carole E. *The Belly Gunner*. New York: 21st Century Books, 2001.

Lee-Brown, Nicole, and Patrick Lee-Brown, eds. *Writers in Britain: Poets of the First World War*. London: Evans Brothers Ltd., 2002.

McGowen, Tom. *World War I* (First Book). New York: Franklin Watts, 1993.

Rice, Earle, Jr. *The First Battle of the Marne* (Battles That Changed the World). Philadelphia: Chelsea House Publishers, 2002.

Robson, Pam. *All About the First World War (1914–1918)*. London: Hodder and Stoughton, 2003.

Wrenn, Andrew. *The First World War.* Cambridge, England: Cambridge University Press, 1997.

Zeinert, Karen. *Those Extraordinary Women of World War I*. Brookfield, CT: Millbrook Press, 2001.

ANNOTATED BIBLIOGRAPHY

Clowes, Peter. "Nurse Edith Clavell." *Military History Magazine*, August 1996 (http://womenshistory.about.com/ library/prm/bledithcavell3.htm). Copyright © 2002 Primedia History Group, a division of Primedia Special Interest Publications. Reprinted with permission.
The About.com site has a section on famous women throughout history, with links to other related sources.

Cowley, Robert, ed. *The Great War: Perspectives on the First World War*. New York: Random House, 2003.
A compilation of thirty articles that shows insight into some of the war's most famous moments, as well as information about how terms and rumors originated.

Duffy, Michael. *Who's Who: Alfred von Schlieffen* (http:// www.firstworldwar.com/bio/schieffen.htm).
This Web site has biographies and primary documents.

Duffy, Michael. *Who's Who: Erich Ludendorff* (http:// www.firstworldwar.com/bio/ludendorff.htm).

Duffy, Michael. *Who's Who: Paul von Hindenburg* (http:// www.firstworldwar.com/bio/hindenburg.htm).

Eisenhower, John S. *Yanks: The Epic Story of the American Army in World War I*. New York: Free Press, 2001.

Figes, Orlando. "The Bread Riot." *The Great War*, PBS (http:// www.pbs.org/greatwar/interviews/figes4.html).

Hendrick, Burton J. *The Life and Letters of Walter H. Page* (http://www.lib.byu.edu/~rdh/wwi/memoir/Page/ PageTC.htm). New York: Doubleday, Page and Co., 1923.

A collection of information and documents about Walter
Page. The book won the Pulitzer Prize in 1923.

Hossack, Anthony R. "Memoirs & Diaries: The First Gas
Attack." *Everyman at War*. Edited by C. B. Purdom.
Unknown publisher, 1930.

Howard, Sir Michael. *The Lessons of History*. Oxford, England:
Oxford University Press, 1991.

Huebner, Captain Henry. "A Memoir of Service in the
German Army During August 1914." *Source Records of
the Great War, Volume II*. Edited by Charles F. Horne.
Publisher unknown (http://www.firstworldwar.com/
diaries/huebner_memoir.htm).

Jevtic, Borijove. "28 June, 1914: The Assassination of
Archduke Franz Ferdinand." World War I Document
Archive (http://www.lib.byu.edu/~rdh/wwi/ferddead.html).

Keegan, John. *The First World War*. New York: Knopf, 1999.
A comprehensive book that looks at many aspects of the
war from one of the best historians in the field.

Lewis, Jon E., et al. "Introduction." *True World War I Stories*.
Guilford, CT: Lyons Press, 2001.
An anthology of eyewitness accounts of being in World War I.

Lodge, Henry Cabot. Speech to the U.S. Senate. August 12, 1919
(http://www.firstworldwar.com/source/
lodge_leagueofnations.htm).

Millet, Allan R. "Bellau Wood: One Man's Initiation." *In Many a
Strife: General Gerald C. Thomas and the U.S. Marine Corps,
1917–1956*. Annapolis, MD: United States Naval Institute
Press, 1993.

"On 'Loving Thine Enemy.'" *The Literary Digest*, March 13, 1915.

"An Open Letter Published in American Newspapers by
Leading German Citizens." *Source Records of the Great
War, Volume II*. Edited by Charles F. Horne. Publisher
unknown (http://www.firstworldwar.com/source/
germanappealtoamericans.htm).

Firstworldwar.com has many original documents and firsthand accounts of the war experience.

Richman, Sheldon. "The Roots of World War II." The Future of
Freedom Foundation. February 1995 (http://www.fff.org/
freedom/0295d.asp).

Scott, Emmett J. *Scott's Official History of the American Negro in
the World War*. Publisher unknown, 1919 (http://
www.lib.byu.edu/~rdh/ww1/comment/scott/scottTC.htm).

This historical document was written by Emmett J. Scott,
the special adjutant to the secretary of war and former
secretary to Booker T. Washington.

Sellman, James Clyde. "African Americans Join the Military."
Encarta Africana (http://www.africana.com/research/
encarta/www1blacks.asp).

Encarta Africana specializes in African American history,
with a special section called the Black Soldiers Resource
Center.

"A Speech to Congress by Senator Robert 'Fightin' Bob' La
Follette." *Words That Changed America*. Edited by Alex
Barnett. Guilford, CT: Lyons Press, 2003.

A collection of speeches throughout history that have had
a strong impact on people and the course of events.

"Telegram from the American Consulate General in Petrograd to the U.S. Secretary of State," March 20, 1917. Hanover Historical Texts Project (http://history.hanover.edu/texts/tel2.html).

Unattributed Primary Documents from Archduke Franz Ferdinand's Assassination, June 28, 1914 (http://www.firstworldwar.com/source/harrachmemoir.htm).

Weintraub, Stanley. *Silent Night: The Story of the World War I Christmas Truce*. New York: Free Press, 2001.
An in-depth look at that mysterious night when weapons were put away and Christmas carols were sung.

Willcox, Alfred. "A July Day at St. Julien." *Everyman at War*. Edited by C. B Purdom. Publisher unknown, 1930 (http://www.firstworldwar.com/diaries/julydayjulien.htm). This Web site is full of firsthand accounts and original documents from the war.

Williams, Nate. "German-Americans in World War I" (http://www.wfa-usa.org/new/germanamer.htm).

Wilson, Woodrow. A Proclamation Issued to the American People. April 15, 1917 (http://www.firstworldwar.com/source/doyourbit.htm).

Winter, Jay, and Blaine Baggett. *The Great War and the Shaping of the 20th Century*. New York: Penguin, 1996.
A companion to the PBS video special, this book takes a look at all aspects of the war, and includes photographs.

INDEX

About the Editor

Tamra Orr is a full-time writer living in Portland, Oregon. She earned a B.A. degree in English and education from Ball State University. She has written a number of nonfiction books for young people and families, including *School Violence: Halls of Hope, Halls of Fear*, *Ronald Reagan: Portrait of an American Hero*, and *The Parent's Guide to Homeschooling*. She has been married to her husband, Joseph, for twenty-two years, and they have four children, ranging in ages from eight to twenty. Writing is her passion because she says it teaches her something new every single day.

Photo Credits

Cover, p. 1 © Hulton Archive/Getty Images, Inc.

Designer: Thomas Forget; Series Editor: Mark Beyer